Joseph Brye is Professor of Music, in charge of Music Theory, and teaches piano at Oregon State University. He previously taught at Stephens College, and the University of Idaho. A Past President of the Oregon Music Teachers Association, Professor Brye is a member of the Western Division and National Executive Board, and National Chairman of College Student Activities and the Constitution and Bylaws Committee of the Music Teachers National Association. He is also President of the Corvallis—Oregon State University Music Association. Professor Brye has published several pieces of his choral music under the auspices of Oregon State University.

BASIC PRINCIPLES

THE RONALD PRESS

OF MUSIC THEORY

JOSEPH BRYE

Oregon State University

COMPANY · NEW YORK

Library of Congress Catalog Card Number: 65–17088

PRINTED IN THE UNITED STATES OF AMERICA

PREFACE

The purpose of this work is to present the basic principles of music theory in a manner which will enable the music student to develop an awareness and an understanding of the materials found in music of the eighteenth and nineteenth centuries. It is designed to be used as a text for first and second year college level music theory classes and may be used in an integrated theory program or for a separate course in harmony.

Each phase of the work is presented so the student will learn to sing, recognize, write, and, above all, think what he hears. The assignments at the conclusion of each chapter develop from a simple manipulation of the materials presented, through their more flexible use, the analysis of musical excerpts containing these same materials, and finally, creative work involving these ideas. Although the basis of this book is that of four-part music, there is ample opportunity to analyze and write in other harmonic arrangements. Numerous excerpts from the standard repertory as well as examples of twentieth-century composition are included to illustrate particular points under discussion, and it is hoped that entire works should be heard whenever possible so the excerpt in question can be studied in context.

While no text in this field can be entirely new or different, the following ideas indicate a partial departure from the typical music theory textbook:

Keyboard Work. Each keyboard assignment is divided into one for the pianist and one for the non-pianist. This is done so the pianist will be challenged and the non-pianist will be able to play what is expected of him with confidence. The instructor will determine the proficiency level of the "pianist" in his class. A suggested level for the "pianist" might be his ability to read simple accompaniments, to play the Bach Two-Part Inventions or the easier Mozart or Haydn Sonatas, and technical control at the four-octave level.

Non-harmonic Tones. Non-harmonic tones are introduced one to a chapter, the first appearing just after part writing is begun. In this procedure the simplest harmonizations can be enhanced and the attention will be focused on one non-harmonic tone at a time.

Melody Writing. The early introduction of melody writing brings the student into contact with the horizontal aspect of music while he is learning the basic harmonic structure. Included in this phase is the study of simple form, rhythm, and accompaniment figures.

Part Writing. As an outgrowth of the study of melody, two- and three-part writing and finally two types of four-part writing are introduced. Here the student may experiment with practical applications of theory in vocal ensembles and instrumental combinations of various types. This phase of the work is developed concurrently with the chorale and keyboard style of harmonization.

Summary of Notation. To insure a knowledge of the simple elements of notation the first section of Chapter 1 briefly defines these elements. This material may be covered rapidly, but the understanding of it must never be taken for granted.

The material in this book is presented in an organized sequence so that the learning process will be logical and meaningful. The first three chapters consist of the study of music fundamentals, which work must be mastered before the student may proceed. In this area the music student is usually the least prepared.

The order of presentation has been tested in the classroom with successful results. The instructor, however, may wish to use the following alternative plan: If he wishes to present the secondary triads immediately after the primary triads rather than delay the study of these chords until after the dominant seventh chord has been presented, the first half of Chapter 9 (up to the secondary triads in the first inversion) may be presented between Chapter 5 and Chapter 6. A special group of exercises is included at the end of Chapter 9 for students following this order.

In endeavoring to make the text complete the author has tried to allow freedom to the imagination and originality of the individual instructor, whose responsibility it is to show the interrelation of the study of music theory to actual music.

Grateful thanks and acknowledgments are due Mr. Robert Walls, Miss Mary Ann Megale, Mr. Ted Mesang, Mr. Ted Carlson, and the music theory students, all of Oregon State University, for their helpfulness and thoughtful criticism of the manuscript.

JOSEPH BRYE

Corvallis, Oregon
April, 1965

CONTENTS

v

BASIC PRINCIPLES
OF MUSIC THEORY

1

NOTATION, SCALES, KEYS

Example 1–1. BEETHOVEN, Sonata, Op. 49, No. 1.

As a point of departure for our study of music theory let us observe the above musical excerpt, which consists of the first eight measures of the first movement of the Beethoven Sonata, Op. 49, No. 1, for piano. The purpose of this observation is to discover some basic elements of notation which are found on a page of printed music.

This segment of a musical composition, as we now see it, is not music. Music is *sound*. Music must be *heard* to exist. What we see above is a systematic grouping of symbols representing sounds, which, when understood and reproduced as sounds, results in what we know as music.

From this example the following elements are observed.

THE GREAT STAFF

This staff, on which music is written, consists of eleven lines and ten spaces constituting the treble staff (higher in pitch) and the bass staff (lower in pitch). The middle or sixth line is omitted, although added when needed, leaving two groups of five lines each. Omission of the sixth line makes it easier to distinguish one line or space from another. The middle line represents "middle C" on the piano.

Example 1–2.

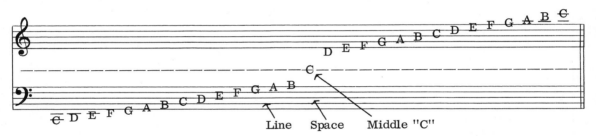

NOTES AND RESTS

A *note* is a symbol representing (a) a musical sound having a definite pitch and (b) the length of time that sound is to be sustained.

A *rest* represents the duration of silence within a musical structure. Example 1–3 is a table of notes and the rests which correspond to them in time value.

Example 1–3.

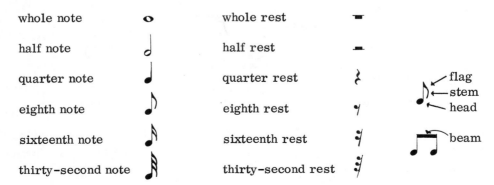

whole note	○	whole rest	▬
half note	♩	half rest	▬
quarter note	♩	quarter rest	𝄽
eighth note	♪	eighth rest	𝄾
sixteenth note	♬	sixteenth rest	𝄿
thirty-second note	♬	thirty-second rest	𝅀

Example 1–4 shows that the relationship of these note and time values is a duple one, each note or rest being divisible by two.

Example 1–4.

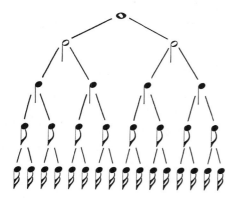 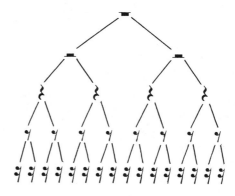

CLEF SIGNS

The treble, or "G," clef usually designates the notes above middle C. G is found on the second line.

The bass, or "F," clef usually designates the notes below middle C. F is found on the fourth line.

Example 1–5.

Treble
sign begins on G   middle C

Bass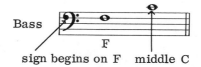
sign begins on F   middle C

METER OR TIME SIGNATURE

This symbol indicates the general feeling of pulse or accent in music. First, to clarify terms, a "measure" is a group of beats or counts, the first of which is normally accented or stressed, whereas a "bar-line" separates one measure from another. The $\frac{2}{4}$ designated in the Beethoven excerpt means that there are (a) two beats per measure, as shown by the numerator, and that (b) a quarter note receives one beat, as indicated by the denominator.

Similarly, $\frac{3}{8}$ would indicate three beats to a measure with an eighth note receiving one beat; or, stated another way, three eighth notes or their equivalent per measure.

NOTE: The time signature has nothing to do with the speed or tempo of the music, but only with the placement of the basic accents.

Example 1–6.

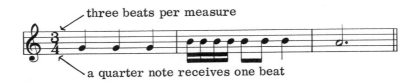

KEY SIGNATURE

A key signature consists of an arrangement of sharps or flats (see "Accidentals" below) appearing on lines and spaces of the staff immediately to the right of the clef signs. These sharps or flats indicate a tonal center or "key" of the composition; the reasons for this will be explained later. The flats on B and E in the treble and bass clef in Example 1–1 represent the key signature in this particular composition.

ACCIDENTALS

These are symbols used on the staff in the body of a composition to raise or lower a note not so designated in the key signature. The "natural," indicated in Example 1–7, cancels any of the other four accidentals.

Example 1–7.

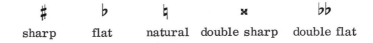

DOTTED NOTES

A dot appearing after a note gives that note half again its original time value.

Example 1–8.

NOTE STEMS

When writing a single note or melody, the stem of the note will go *down* on the *left side* of the note-head if the note is located above the middle line of the staff. The stem will go *up* on the *right side* of the note-head if the note is located below the middle line of the staff. If the note is located on the middle line, the stem will go down, unless the other notes in the group or measure are located below the middle line.

Example 1–9.

THE SLUR

This is a curved line placed over or under two or more notes of different pitches to indicate that they are to be played *legato* (in a smooth, connected manner) or sung with one breath. A slur that connects two notes having the same pitch is called a "tie," the two notes sounding as one, with the combined time value of both.

Example 1–10.

FLAGS OR BEAMS

Groups of two or more notes with flags (eighths, sixteenths, etc.) are notated in two ways. (a) In vocal music where each note represents a different syllable to be sung, the flag is used for each note. (b) In piano and other instrumental music, as well as in vocal music where more than one note is sung with the same syllable, the beam is used. Beams are also used to group notes by measures or beats and to indicate an irregular grouping of notes.

Example 1–11. ENGLISH FOLK SONG, Early One Morning.

Example 1–12. BEETHOVEN, Sonata, Op. 14, No. 2 (Scherzo).

TEMPO INDICATIONS

"Andante," at the beginning of the Beethoven excerpt (Example 1–1), is an indication of the rate of speed and manner of playing for this work. Because the universal language for musical terms is Italian, it is possible to understand the terms used on printed music of different countries and periods by learning a few Italian words. Occasionally, composers will write these indications in their own language; Brahms wrote in German, Debussy, in French, and some American composers write in English. These, however, are exceptions. In the "Glossary of Musical Terms" (page 266), the most frequently used tempo indications are defined.

DYNAMICS INDICATIONS

Individual letters, such as the *"p"* in the Beethoven example, are used to indicate degrees of volume of sound (loudness or softness). These indications are also defined in the "Glossary of Musical Terms."

Scales

Before scales and keys are discussed, something should be known of their purpose. When music is heard, there is an awareness on the part of the listener of a relationship of tones to each other and of groups of tones to the entire composition. This has been true throughout the evolution of music, and, although styles have developed and changed, there still remains a relationship of parts with the whole. This relationship has to do with scales and keys—with the feeling of tonality. An exception to this would be found in some twentieth-century music, in which there is a strikingly different relationship of tones and in which a feeling of key is often avoided.

Our ears accept certain combinations of sounds as being correct, beautiful, or at least belonging to each other, and our likes and dislikes are tempered by the society in which we live and by the period in which we are living.

A *scale* is a succession of musical tones, usually arranged in half and whole steps and forming a particular pattern. The word "scale" is derived from the Latin *"scala,"* meaning "ladder." Actually, as it appears to the eye and sounds to the ear, the scale does resemble a ladder.

A *half step* is the interval between one tone and its closest neighbor, to the right or left, on the piano keyboard. The interval from a white key to an adjacent black key, or vice versa, is a half step, as is the distance between two white keys with no black key between. The half step is the smallest division of sound used in the music of our western culture. Although experiments are being conducted by some composers in the use of other divisions of the whole tone, such as the quarter tone, these must be considered largely experimental at present.

A *whole step* consists of two half steps.

The Major Scale

STRUCTURE

The major scale consists of consecutive tones (half and whole steps) from one letter name to its repetition above or below, such as C D E F G A B C, in which all are whole steps except those from

E to F (3 to 4) and B to C (7 to 8) in the succession, which are half steps. This is called a "diatonic" scale, because the scale steps follow the letter names in succession without alteration and include five whole steps and two half steps in a definite pattern.

This pattern may easily be seen by observing on the keyboard the arrangement of black and white keys between C and the C above it. By playing only the white keys from one C to the next C the C major scale has been constructed. Here the half steps between 3 and 4 and between 7 and 8 are obvious, because there are no black keys present to place two half steps between them.

Example 1–13.

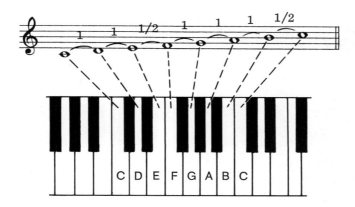

By following this pattern of whole and half steps, it is possible to construct a major scale from any given note, providing each letter name is used, in alphabetical order, in the scale.

MEDIEVAL MODES

A number of diatonic scale formations are possible, the major scale described above being one of them. In medieval music these scale formations were known as "modes," and each had its own arrangement of whole and half steps. Some contemporary composers have returned to these modes as a melodic and harmonic basis for their compositions. These medieval modes are written in Example 1–14, each using the white keys of the piano but each having a different starting note. Note that the Ionian mode is our present-day major scale.

Example 1–14.

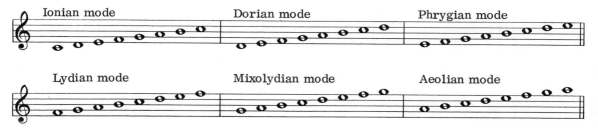

Keys and Key Signatures

KEY

In the harmonic sense, a key consists of a group of related tones which are drawn to a dominating tone called the "keynote." In the key of C major, the keynote is C. Flats or sharps are needed to construct any major scale except that of C major.

Example 1–15.

KEY SIGNATURE

A grouping of sharps or flats necessary to make the scale conform to the pattern of whole and half steps is called the key signature. It is placed at the beginning of each staff, following the clef sign, and is to be used throughout the composition unless otherwise indicated. The use of the key signature eliminates the tedious task of writing sharps or flats before each note to be raised or lowered. The only instances in which a key signature is not used is in certain contemporary music which is atonal (having no key center), or in which the key center changes so frequently that the composer feels a key signature is superfluous. Check the key signature in the Beethoven excerpt (Example 1–1) at the beginning of this chapter.

KEY SIGNATURE PATTERN

The vertical and horizontal arrangement of sharps in a key signature is illustrated in Example 1–16. In a major key the right-hand sharp is the seventh step of the scale, so the keynote is located one half step above this right sharp.

Example 1–16.

The arrangement of flats in a key signature is illustrated in Example 1–17. In a major key the right-hand flat is the fourth step of the scale, so the keynote is located by counting up to 8 from 4 or down to 1 from 4. An easy way of learning these major flat key signatures is to remember that the keynote is the same as the flat next to the right-hand flat.

Example 1–17.

It is obvious that there is a definite pattern involved in the placing of sharps and flats in the key signature. The next sharp to be added in the key signature is found by counting up to the fifth letter name from the preceding one (F G A B C). In the arrangement of sharps the pattern of "down 4 and up 5" from the first sharp constitutes an upward movement. A sharp and B sharp are placed an octave (eight scale steps) lower than the pattern would suggest so that the sharps will remain on the staff.

In major keys involving flats the next flat in order is found by counting up to the fourth letter name (B C D E). A flat lowers a note, so the pattern of flats from the first one is "up 4 and down 5," which is moving in a downward direction.

The Circle of Fifths

TETRACHORDS

If we observe closely the pattern of whole and half steps in the major scale, we notice that there are two identical patterns within the scale. Each pattern consists of four notes with the structure of two whole steps plus a half step. A whole step separates the two groups. These four-note groups are known as "tetrachords."

Example 1–18.

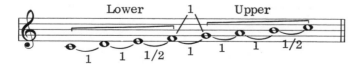

The upper tetrachord in the scale of C begins on G and is the lower tetrachord in the scale of G. Similarly, the upper tetrachord in the scale of G is the lower tetrachord in the scale of D with one more sharp in the key signature, and so on.

Example 1–19.

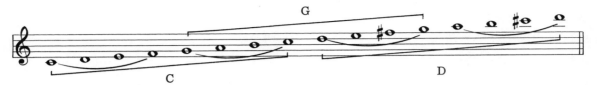

SEQUENCE OF KEYS

By continuing this succession of tetrachords, each beginning a fifth above the other (counting the keynote as 1), it is possible to go completely through all of the major keys and arrive back at the key of C. The diagram in Example 1–20, in the form of a circle, illustrates the connection of one major key with another and the relationship of keys with one more (or less) sharp or flat. Several keys may be considered to use either sharps or flats. These are called "enharmonic" keys because, whether sharps or flats are used in the key signature, the key will be the same in sound.

Knowledge of the key relationships found in Example 1–20 will become more valuable as the student works with these various keys.

Example 1–20.

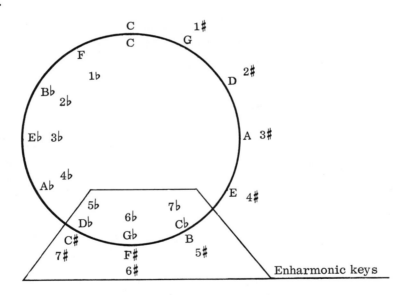

The Minor Scales

The minor mode or scale form is actually the Aeolian mode of medieval times (see page 9); the Aeolian mode and the Ionian mode (our present major scale) are the only medieval modes which have been in general use since the Renaissance. The minor mode creates a different impression from the major, because of the difference in the arrangement of the whole and half steps.

There are three forms of the minor scale, and each has its own function. These are the *natural* or pure minor, the *harmonic* minor, and the *melodic* minor.

THE NATURAL MINOR

In this form of the minor scale the half steps occur between 2 and 3 and between 5 and 6, the others being whole steps. This pattern will become clear if we observe on the keyboard the arrangement of the white keys from A to the A above it. Here is the "a minor" scale in the natural form, with the half steps clearly indicated. This is the basic minor form, and we will use it as our point of departure in writing music and as an aid in the construction of the other forms.

Example 1–21.

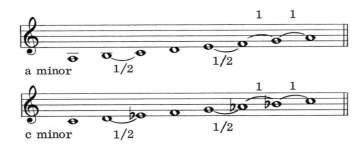

THE HARMONIC MINOR

This form differs from the natural form only in regard to the *seventh step* or scale degree. Here the seventh degree is raised a half step, thereby resulting in one whole and one half step between 6 and 7, and one half step between 7 and 8. This half step between 7 and 8 creates a driving force in music, and its presence helps to establish the key and stimulate motion. In the major mode there is a half step between 7 and 8, giving the seventh step this urgency to move to the keynote. We are accustomed to hearing this and normally prefer its sound to that of a whole step between these two tones. This form has value from the standpoint of basic chord structure, as we will discover later.

Example 1–22.

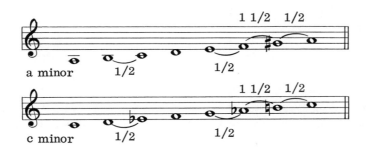

THE MELODIC MINOR

As the name suggests, this form is used mainly to produce a smoother melodic feeling than can be achieved by the use of the step and a half between 6 and 7 in the harmonic form, while maintaining the half step between 7 and 8. The melodic form is the same as the natural form but with two exceptions: (a) the sixth and seventh degrees are raised when ascending, thereby producing a whole step between 6 and 7 and the desired half step between 7 and 8, and (b) the sixth and seventh degrees are lowered to the natural form when descending. Note that the upper tetrachord of the ascending melodic minor scale is identical with the upper tetrachord of the major scale.

Example 1–23.

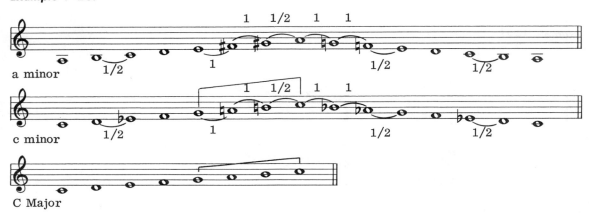

The lower tetrachord of all three forms of minor is identical. The real character of the minor mode in general is based on the fact that the third of the scale is lowered from the major scale.

Relationship of Major and Minor

There are two basic relationships between major and minor, the one dealing with the key signature and the other with the keynote. The natural form of the minor scale is used to illustrate this relationship.

RELATIVE MINOR

The relationship here is one of key signature. Play a major scale from keynote to keynote, then begin again on the *sixth step* of that scale and play the same notes up to the recurrence of the sixth step. This second scale would be a minor scale in the natural form, and would be called the "relative" minor of the major scale played first. The keynote of the minor scale would be that of the sixth step of the major scale. The same flats or sharps would be used for both of these scales, so the key signature would remain the same.

Example 1–24.

The key signature for a composition in a minor key is determined by (a) naming the major key from the key signature, then (b) finding the minor keynote and thus the minor key, which would be the sixth step of that major scale. If the signature is not given, but only a name such as "e minor," remember that e is the sixth step in the major scale having the same key signature (or count up three half steps to find that major key).

Example 1–25.

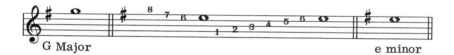

PARALLEL MINOR

This relationship, sometimes called "tonic minor," deals with the keynote. Play a major scale from keynote to keynote; then begin again *on the same keynote,* but this time play a scale using the arrangement of whole and half steps fitting the natural minor form. You will discover that the letter names of the scale degrees are the same and the keynote is the same, but accidentals are required to complete the minor form. This minor scale is the "parallel" minor of the major scale played first. The keynote is the same but the key signature is different.

This parallel minor relationship is frequently used where an interchange of mode is desired, as between C major and c minor. Although the key signatures are different, a major key and its parallel minor key are nearly identical, because it is possible to pass from one to the other with change of color and added interest, yet with no change of key actually taking place. This interchange of mode will be studied in more detail in Chapter 15.

Example 1–26.

IMPORTANT: All three forms of the minor scale (natural, harmonic, and melodic) may be used with either of the above relationships, because relative and parallel here refer specifically to the relationship of minor with major, not with the actual structure of the scales.

The Chromatic Scale

This scale consists of all of the half steps in succession from one keynote to the next. This is not an independent scale, but is actually derived from the major scale, with half steps being inserted between the whole steps. It is used primarily for melodic purposes where the alteration of scale degrees is desired. In the ascending chromatic scale it is the general practice to raise the diatonic scale steps and in the descending chromatic scale to lower them.

Example 1–27.

Assignments

1. Select and copy a page of manuscript, practicing the writing of notes, rests, and clef signs for neatness and legibility.

2. Identify the following notes for pitch and time value:

3. Place bar lines correctly to conform with the time signature in the following:
   (a)

   (b)

4. Bring some printed music to class and discuss the application of the elements presented in the early part of this chapter to the music.

5. Construct a major scale, on paper or at the piano, from any given note in either the treble or bass clef.

   NOTE: Non-pianists should play these scales in tetrachords (see page 11) using four fingers of both the left and right hands (no thumbs). If playing scales following the circle of 5ths, begin the new scale with the upper tetrachord of the previous scale. Pianists should play these scales with both hands together and with accepted scale fingerings.

6. Write the following key signatures in both clefs:

   (a) B flat major   (f) f minor
   (b) c sharp minor   (g) D flat major
   (c) g sharp minor   (h) A major
   (d) E flat major   (i) b minor
   (e) e minor   (j) C sharp major

7. Write all three forms of the scale of b flat minor in both clefs, using accidentals, not key signatures.

8. Write the D major scale, then write its parallel and relative minor scales, using key signatures and the harmonic form of the minor scale, in both clefs.

9. Play all forms of the minor scale in a key given by the instructor, and explain the differences among these forms.

10. Practice singing the major scale and the three forms of the minor scale. First sing these from keynote to keynote, then start on any degree of the scale and go either up or down. Use neutral syllables (la, la), numbers representing the scale degrees, letter names, or the *solfège* system (do, re, mi, etc.), depending on the wishes of the instructor.

11. Examine well-known musical compositions, preferably those being studied, to determine the key in which the composition is written. If written in a minor key, study the possible adaptation of the different forms.

2

INTERVALS

An *interval* is a combination of two tones. It is also the distance between or the difference between two tones. When these two tones are sounded together the result is an *harmonic* interval, and when they are sounded one after the other the result is a *melodic* interval. The quality of an interval is determined by its size and by the relationship of its position to the keynote.

IDENTIFICATION

An interval is named according to the number of scale steps it encompasses, counting the first note as 1. Thus, from C up to E would be an interval of a third.

Example 2–1.

MARPURG, Menuet.

18

An interval may be reckoned either up or down; to begin with, we will reckon up. "Unison" or "prime" is the term given to the same tone sounded simultaneously or successively in two voices. "Octave" is the term given to an interval of an eighth, such as from F to the next F.

Example 2–2.

STRUCTURE

Considering the lower note of the intervals as a *temporary* keynote and using the upper notes as they appear in a major scale, examine Example 2–3. Notice that the unison, fourth, fifth, and octave are called "perfect," and that the second, third, sixth, and seventh are called "major." Unisons, fourths, fifths, and octaves, as well as chords built on the first, fourth, and fifth degrees of the scale have a prominent place in the study of music, and because of their nature and function are, in a sense, set apart.

The lower note of an interval will seldom be the keynote, but this illustration is for the sake of presenting these intervals in a manner that is easy to understand. One might determine the number of whole and half steps involved in each interval, which would be a good procedure for seconds and thirds, but this would become a tedious method for the other intervals.

Example 2–3.

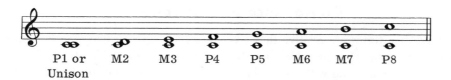

TYPES

There are five types of intervals: major (indicated by M), minor (m), perfect (P), diminished (dim.), and augmented (Aug.).

A *major* interval contracted—by lowering the upper note or raising the lower note—by one half step becomes *minor*, and contracted by another half step becomes *diminished*.

A *perfect* interval contracted by a half step becomes *diminished*, and contracted by another half step (not usually practical), becomes *doubly diminished*.

A *perfect* or a *major* interval expanded by a half step becomes *augmented*. In regard to the size of intervals and their names, Example 2–4 shows the only way in which perfect and major intervals are similar.

Example 2–4.

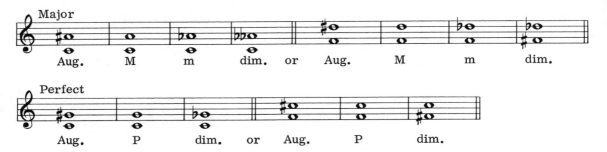

NOTE: Until intervals can be easily recognized, one might consider the bottom note as a *temporary* keynote as was suggested earlier, then adjust either upper or lower note to form a familiar interval, and finally, determine the exact interval by the contraction or expansion caused by the flats or sharps.

Example 2–5.

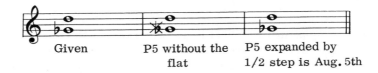

Consonance and Dissonance

Because these two terms are relative they have undergone great changes in interpretation in the history of harmonic music, changes which are still taking place today. The terms "consonance" and "dissonance" have nothing to do with sounds being pleasing or harsh, but deal instead with a sense of motion within the musical context. All music represents a combination of an urgency to move and a feeling of stability, the development of tension and the release of this tension—the same factors that are a part of our everyday living.

These opposing forces are present even in a simple melody where a combination of active and rest tones produces the interest. Both of these factors are needed to stimulate movement and development of an idea. This aspect of active and rest tones is discussed under "Melody and Rhythm" in Chapter 4.

CONSONANCE

A sound which is stable and which does not have the urgency to resolve is called a consonance. This term refers to chords as well as to intervals. The consonant intervals are: all perfect intervals (except the perfect fourth in certain instances) and the major and minor thirds and sixths.

These are divided into two groups, the perfect and imperfect consonances, their placement being determined by their degree of stability.

The *perfect consonances* are the perfect unisons, octaves, fifths, and fourths (the fourth is considered a perfect consonance only when there is a third or a perfect fifth below it).

The *imperfect consonances* are the major and minor thirds and sixths.

Example 2–6.

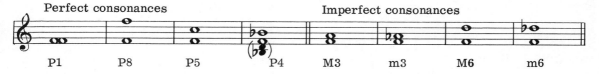

DISSONANCE

A sound which is unstable, more active, and which needs to resolve to a consonant interval is called a dissonance. The dissonant intervals are as follows: the augmented and diminished intervals, the major and minor seconds and sevenths, and the perfect fourth, when not supported by a third or a perfect fifth below it. These are arranged in Example 2–7 from the milder to the stronger dissonances.

Example 2–7.

NOTE: Example 2–7 represents the accepted classifications of the relative stability of intervals. However, in musical compositions the degree of stability of an interval tends to vary because of the context. The study and use of consonance and dissonance represents one of the main driving forces in music and will be dealt with in more detail later. More and more sounds which at one time were considered dissonant are now at least approaching the realm of consonance. Contemporary composers who write in the atonal style, that is, with no tonal center or keynote feeling, go to the extreme of denying the existence of dissonance.

Inversion of Intervals

HARMONIC INVERSION

Of the two types of inversion, this is the type that affects the size and type of interval. An interval is inverted harmonically by transferring its lower note into the higher octave or its higher note into the lower octave. A perfect interval when inverted remains perfect, a major interval becomes minor and vice versa, and an augmented interval becomes diminished, and vice versa. Notice in Example 2–8 that the number of the original interval plus the number of the inversion always equals nine.

Example 2–8.

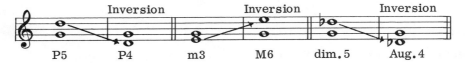

MELODIC INVERSION

This type, also known as the "mirror-type" inversion, is used primarily in the development of a musical idea. It is a standard device in writing fugues, such as those by Bach, and is also used in the twelve-tone technique, as found in the works of Arnold Schoenberg and his followers. As the name suggests, melodic inversion consists of changing each ascending interval into a corresponding descending interval and vice versa. Except in atonal music, where the exact interval is used in the inversion, the inverted interval usually follows the scale steps within the key.

Example 2–9.

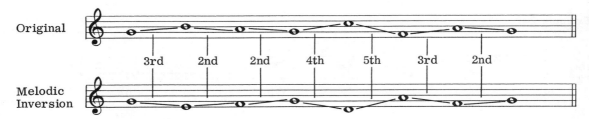

Compound Intervals

Compound intervals encompass *more* than an octave. An octave and one step is called a ninth and an octave and two steps is called a tenth, but usually beyond a tenth the actual interval, disregarding the octave, is used. For example, an eleventh would be called a fourth, except in certain isolated cases to be discussed later. The type of interval (major, minor, etc.) remains the same, as though the octave had not been added.

Example 2–10.

Enharmonic Intervals

Enharmonic intervals are those which sound the same but are written differently (see enharmonic keys, page 12). For example, F sharp on the piano sounds the same as G flat, but the two are written as different notes. In regard to intervals, a diminished fifth sounds the same as an augmented fourth, but the notation is different—these are enharmonic intervals. The decision to use one or the other of these intervals is dependent on voice-leading and key, and will become clear when chord progression is discussed.

Example 2–11.

NOTE: The knowledge of intervals is of tremendous importance in the study, performance, and composing of music. It is imperative that one be able to recognize, sing, and write all intervals correctly and with ease. Because each phase in the study of music theory is dependent on what has been learned in the preceding chapters, it is essential to understand each phase of the work as it is presented.

Assignments

1. Identify the following intervals:
   (a)

   (b)

2. Construct the following intervals above the given note:

3. Construct the following intervals below the given note:

    m6   Aug. 4   M7   P4   dim. 5   m3   M6   dim. 7   P5   M3

4. Listen to intervals as they are played and write the size and type of each. When the upper or lower note is given, write the interval on the staff.

5. Invert the following intervals harmonically, either up or down, and label each interval and its inversion:

6. Label the intervals below, then write and label the enharmonic equivalent of the intervals, changing the notation of one or both of the notes in the interval.

7. Practice singing all of the intervals studied in this chapter, first starting from the same note, later starting each time from a different note. Practice this first going up from a given note, then going down.

NOTE: At the beginning it may be easier to associate a particular interval with the beginning of some familiar song, to set the interval in the mind.

8. Determine the intervals in a familiar melody as to consonance or dissonance, and label them. Make a similar study of an angular melody of the twentieth century; after you have analyzed it, sing the melody, interval by interval—very slowly.

3

TRIADS: FORMS AND FUNCTIONS

CHORD

A chord is a combination of several, usually three or more, tones sounded together. If they are sounded separately, but in a group, they are said to be "broken chords" or "arpeggios." Chord tones are basically arranged in a pattern of successive thirds, although some contemporary composers are using other intervals, such as the fourth, as a basis for the harmonic pattern. Most of the material studied in this text will be based on the music of the eighteenth and nineteenth centuries, called the "common practice" period, so we will not be dealing with any of the more recent idioms until near the end of this study.

18th, 19th cent.
Same working "vocabulary"
Bach to Brahms

TRIAD

A triad is a chord composed of three tones, and consists of two intervals of a third, one above the other. The three tones of the triad are named, from the lowest up, the *root, third,* and *fifth.*

Play middle C on the piano, then play a third higher and another third higher (E and G); the resulting sound is a triad—one of the most basic yet most satisfying sounds in music. There is an acoustical reason for the success and strength of the triad. When a single sound is produced, additional sounds called *overtones* are also produced, but these are not heard as distinctly, because they are less intense than the *fundamental* (the original tone). A bell would illustrate this better than a piano. Overtones are arranged naturally in a definite pattern, which is given in Example 3–1. This is important because the fundamental, C in this example, and the first five overtones constitute the C–E–G triad, which is the mainstay of the key of C major.

Example 3–1.

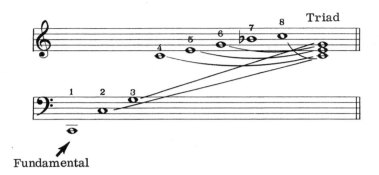

Fundamental

When the triad is arranged so that the third or the fifth is the lowest note, the result is an inversion of the original triad. In Example 3–2 are four different arrangements of the same triad, C–E–G. Each arrangement produces a slightly different effect, but the triad in each case is still the C–E–G triad.

Example 3–2.

NOMENCLATURE

Scale steps and the triads built on these scale steps are labeled with Roman numerals indicating the specific degree of the scale and are also given names which denote the function and placement of the scale step or triad.

I. *Tonic*—or keynote.
II. *Supertonic*—one step above the tonic.
III. *Mediant*—midway between the tonic and the dominant.
IV. *Subdominant*—same distance below the tonic as the dominant is above the tonic.
V. *Dominant*—the dominating factor in the key.
VI. *Submediant*—midway from the tonic down to the subdominant.
VII. *Leading tone*—has an urgency to move up to the tonic. Sometimes called the subtonic.

STRUCTURE OF TRIADS

In analyzing the structure of the triads as they are built on the various degrees of the scale, the size of the triad is determined by the distance between the *root and third* and the *root and fifth* of the triad. In Example 3–3 a triad is built on each of the scale steps of the major scale. Above the staff, the structure of each triad is indicated in terms of the type of third and fifth present.

Example 3-3.

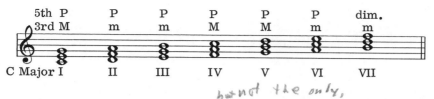

The harmonic form of the minor scale is the basic form used in writing music involving chord structures, but with the following changes and additions:

[handwritten: but not the only, in minor]

1. The mediant triad in the harmonic form is augmented, but this triad in the minor mode is preferred in the unaltered (natural) form.

2. The V and the VII are usually used with the raised leading tone, but may be used without the alteration if a strong leading tone tendency is not desired.

3. Occasionally the IV chord, which is minor in minor keys, is made major by raising the third of the chord, the sixth of the scale. The ascending melodic minor scale form is the basis of this alteration.

4. Other infrequently used changes will be discussed later. Aside from the minor key characteristics, it is possible to alter all triads within major or minor tonalities for a desired effect.

Example 3-4 gives an analysis of triad structure for the minor mode. The triads written in black notes are those which are infrequently used and require special considerations in terms of harmonic and melodic context.

Example 3-4.

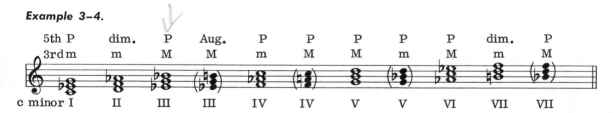

TYPES OF TRIADS

The preceding illustrations show the presence of four types of triads represented in major and minor keys. They are indicated as follows:

1. *Major triad*—major third and perfect fifth. Includes I, IV, and V in a major key, and III, V, VI, and sometimes VII and IV in a minor key.

2. *Minor triad*—minor third and perfect fifth. Includes II, III, and VI in a major key, and I, IV, and sometimes V in a minor key.

3. *Diminished triad*—minor third and diminished fifth. Includes VII in a major key, and II and VII in a minor key.

4. *Augmented triad*—major third and augmented fifth. Includes III in the strict harmonic form of the minor, but is seldom used with this structure.

Example 3-5 will clarify the structure of these four types of triads.

Example 3–5.

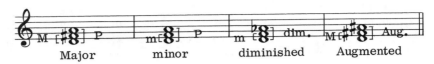

Major   minor   diminished   Augmented

FREQUENCY OF USE

The most commonly used triads are the major and minor, because these sounds represent the basis and background of music and because they contain only consonant intervals. The augmented and diminished triads are used less frequently, because they contain dissonant intervals, the augmented and diminished fifths, and are more limited and specific in their function.

CHORD LABELS

To aid in recognizing the size of the triad from the Roman numeral, the following device is used, but it should be understood that this is arbitrary:

Major: large Roman numeral—I
Minor: small Roman numeral—ii
Diminished: small Roman numeral with degree symbol—vii°
Augmented: large Roman numeral with plus sign—III+

In addition, major keys are designated by a capital letter, as "C" or "C major," while minor keys are designated by a small (lower case) letter, as "c" or "c minor."

PRIMARY AND SECONDARY TRIADS

In Chapter 2 it was observed that intervals, as they appear in a major scale pattern are either major or perfect. Unisons, fourths, fifths, and octaves are perfect; the others, major. A similar distinction is found in the *triads* on each step of the major scale. The triads built on these same scale steps, now known as tonic (I), subdominant (IV), and dominant (V), are major triads in major keys and are called *primary* triads.

The others are less basic, the supertonic (ii), mediant (iii), and submediant (vi) being minor, and the leading tone triad (vii°) being diminished. These are called *secondary* triads. The observation again sets apart the first, fourth, and fifth degrees of the scale and places them in a special category— as red, yellow, and blue remain in a special relationship to the other colors.

Example 3–6.

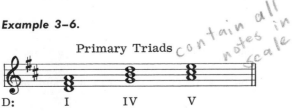

Primary Triads   Secondary Triads

D: I   IV   V   D: ii   iii   vi   vii°

These classifications apply to these triads in both major and minor keys.

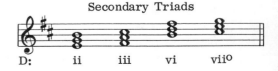

TRIADS IN CONTEXT

Examine the examples below and you will discover that any major, minor, or diminished triad can be interpreted as belonging to more than one key. No alterations are given here except those described on page 27. Any triad has little meaning, except that of its own individual sound, unless placed in the context of a key. Then each is distinctive and becomes vital, because of its relationship to the tonic.

Major Triad. In discussing the types of triads, we observed that the I, IV, and V in major keys and the III, V, VI, and sometimes the IV and VII in minor keys are major triads. A single major triad, then, may be interpreted as belonging to eight possible keys, as follows:

Example 3–7.

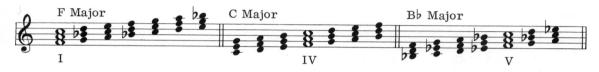

Minor Triad. The same principle may be applied to the minor triads.

Example 3–8.

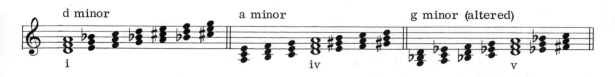

Diminished Triad. The same principle applies here, but in a more limited way.

Example 3-9.

Augmented Triad. Because the augmented triad, even the III⁺, is the result of chromatic altera-tion which is not an integral part of the key, illustrations using this triad would have little value.

Example 3-10 summarizes the key relationships of triads. This procedure can be carried out with any major, minor, diminished, or augmented triad.

Example 3-10.

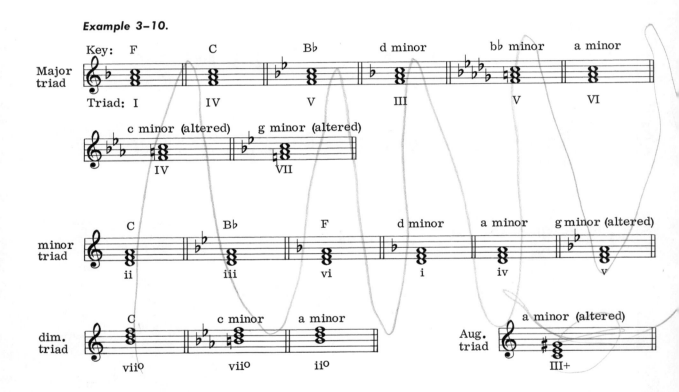

Assignments

1. Learn to recognize the four types of triads when they are played.
2. Learn to sing the four types of triads in these three ways:
   (a) From a given tone, sing the triads, using a neutral syllable.
   (b) From a given named note, sing each of the triads, using letter names.
   (c) From a given third or fifth of each type of triad, sing a pattern including the other two notes as follows, using numbers or letter names:

3. Construct the following triads:

M   dim.   m   Aug.   m   Aug.   M   dim.   m   m

4. Construct the following triads in the bass clef:

m   M   M   dim.   Aug.   dim.   M   Aug.   m   dim.

over

5. Identify the following triads:

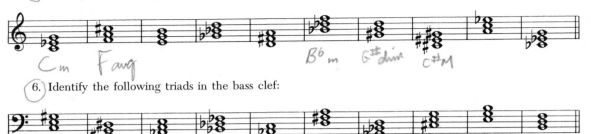

6. Identify the following triads in the bass clef:

7. Write each of the following triads in all possible keys, as in Example 3–10:

8. Play all four types of triads from any given note on the piano, either as isolated triads with no key designation, or as a particular triad in a given key; for example, play the subdominant triad in the key of D flat major, or play III in the key of b minor, using the natural form of the minor.

4
THE PRIMARY TRIADS: TONIC, SUBDOMINANT, DOMINANT

& POSSIBLY SUPERTONIC

To review, the primary triads are those constructed on the first, fourth, and fifth degrees of the scale and are named tonic, subdominant, and dominant, respectively.

In a major key all three are major triads, and in a minor key the tonic and subdominant are minor while the dominant triad usually remains major. The harmonic minor form is used here to create the leading tone tendency of the seventh scale step.

Example 4–1.

These triads represent the three basic sounds in harmonic music, and all other chords are derived, at least to a certain extent, from these three. Because all seven tones of the diatonic scale are

33

found in the three primary triads, it is possible to harmonize any diatonic melody with these three triads. They have been the mainstay of all musical composition from the baroque period up to and including part of the twentieth century.

FUNCTION

Each of the primary triads has a particular function in the tonality or key to which it belongs, as follows:

1. The *tonic* triad (I) gives a feeling of repose, of stability, and creates a sense of completeness in music, because it is the object of all harmonic progression. It also serves as a point of departure; from the tonic one may progress to any other chord in the key. Most compositions begin and end with the tonic chord.

2. The *subdominant* triad (IV) is less stable than the tonic and demands movement. It does, however, include the tonic tone or keynote, which somewhat limits that urgency to move. The natural tendency for the subdominant triad is to move to the tonic in a non-conclusive manner or indirectly (as will be studied later) to the dominant. It is the only primary triad which will harmonize the fourth or sixth scale step in a melody, so it is used mainly to produce movement within a musical framework.

3. The *dominant* triad (V) is very unstable and has a greater tendency to move to the tonic than the subdominant, largely because of the presence of the leading tone in the chord. This leading tone is the most active step in the scale and forces movement to the keynote. The dominant triad is the most valuable one in music and is perhaps the one most frequently used outside of the tonic. It is the chord through which all other chords naturally move in order to arrive eventually at the final tonic triad.

NOTE: Again, it may prove helpful and interesting to notice the correlation between the basic principles of harmony and painting. There are three primary colors, red, yellow, and blue, which are basic and out of which all other colors, with the assistance of black and white, are created. The same is true of the three primary triads in music, the range and tone quality of the sounds corresponding to the addition of black and white. With imagination, one can almost associate a particular color with each triad, because of the difference between them in stability and function.

Four-Part Writing (Chorale Style)

Four voices (parts) will be used in our first experience with writing music using chords, because of the possibilities of variety and also because these four parts represent the hymn tune, which is the basis of choral music, and the string quartet, which is the nucleus of the symphony. Once facility is gained in this style, writing in two and three parts as well as piano style will be introduced.

RANGE

The four voices to be used are soprano, alto, tenor, and bass. The general ranges of these voices are as follows:

Chorale texture (SATB) 2 staves

Piano texture — 3 parts in right hand, one in bass

Example 4–2.

These ranges are for the human voice. If we were writing for instrumental combinations, we would need to know the range of the particular instrument, which may be greater than that of the human voice.

DOUBLING

The doubling of one member of the triad is necessary in order to provide the needed four notes in the chord. The most satisfactory note to double in the I, IV, and V chords is the root; next in preference is the fifth, and least is the third. A more complete discussion of doubling is found in Chapter 7. For the present the *root* will be doubled. — *reinforce its dynamic quality*

In Example 4–3, notice the direction of the *note-stems* in four-part, chorale style writing. The soprano and tenor stems go up and the alto and bass stems go down. This procedure is used for ease in distinguishing each part, and also to facilitate the reading of any one part horizontally without confusion.

Example 4–3.

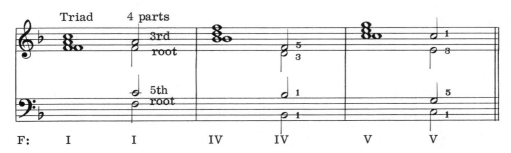

ROOT POSITION

Any chord is in *root* position if the root of the chord is in the bass part. For the present the primary triads will be written only in root position. Example 4–3 illustrates chords in root position.

CLOSE AND OPEN ~~POSITION~~ SPACING

This refers to the placement and spacing of the notes in a chord. In "close" position, no member of the same triad can be inserted between the soprano and alto, or between the alto and tenor voices. In "open" position, a member of the same triad may be inserted between the soprano and alto, and between the alto and tenor.

CLOSE — less than 8ve betw. S & T

Stated another way, in close position there is less than an octave between the soprano and tenor voices, while in open position there is an octave or more between the soprano and tenor voices.

In either close or open position the distance between the tenor and bass may be great or small, depending on the effect desired. It may be well to keep in mind that the lower the range, the thicker the texture, and notes close together in the lower register tend to produce a thick, indistinct sound.

In Example 4–4, each "x" represents a chord tone which might be inserted between two voices.

Example 4–4.

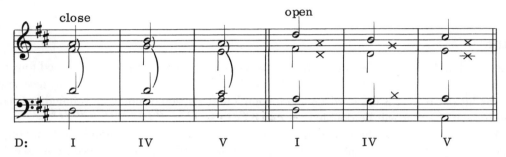

SOPRANO POSITION

The position of the *octave, third,* or *fifth* refers to the note in the triad which is found in the soprano voice. This is not used in the writing of actual music but as a soprano indication at the beginning of given bass parts to be harmonized.

Example 4–5.

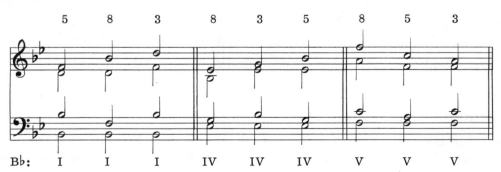

SPACING LIMITS

There must not be, for the present, more than an octave between soprano and alto, and between alto and tenor. There may be, however, more than an octave between tenor and bass. On occasion the same note may be sounded in two adjacent voices, including the bass part.

Example 4-6.

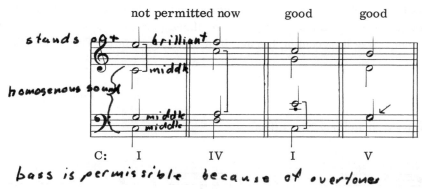

NOTE: These principles of basic four-part writing, as well as all of the principles in this book, are the result of the practice of composers as found in actual music. They serve as a point of departure. While the principles may seem rigid at this point, many of them are quite flexible, and after their strict use is mastered, exceptions will be introduced which will lend variety, interest, and individuality to writing.

Melody and Rhythm

While we seem to be concerned in this course mainly with the study of chord structure and how chords are made to fit together into a meaningful progression, we actually have as our goal the understanding, through study, of the elements and characteristics of music. We need to have just as much understanding of melody and rhythm and the places they hold in music as of chord structure, because without melody and rhythm the arrangements of the chords studied will have little meaning.

NATURE OF MELODY

A melody consists of a succession of tones of varying pitches. These tones are given time values and are arranged in groups by accents, the result being a musical thought. In order to play, sing, or write a melody well, it is essential to observe these points. Examine the following melody:

Example 4-7.

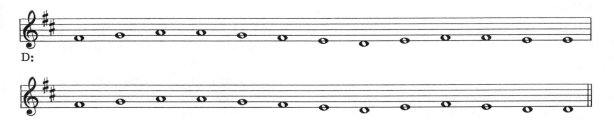

Notice that there are no bar lines, no indication of accent, no variety of time values given the notes—simply a succession of notes. Example 4–8 gives the same melody with a time signature and bar lines to indicate the measures. Now one can feel a rhythmic pulse in this melody and the entire work has musical meaning. Sing it, accenting the first beat of each measure. This is how Beethoven wrote the melody:

Example 4–8. BEETHOVEN, Symphony No. 9 (finale).

Example 4–9 shows the same melody with a different arrangement of accents and a different time signature. Note the difference between this melody and the one just above. How does the shift in accent and grouping affect the melody? Does the melody seem different?

Example 4–9.

ACTIVE AND INACTIVE TONES

Just as music is composed of elements of tension and relaxation, so certain steps in the scale have an urgency to move while others do not. A successful melody has a combination of these two types of steps, resulting in effective forward movement combined with stability.

Active tones within a scale are those which demand movement in a particular direction. They are unstable and create a feeling of pressure which can only be relieved by this resolution. The active tones are 2, 4, 6, and 7 in the scale, and resolve in the following manner:

Example 4–10.

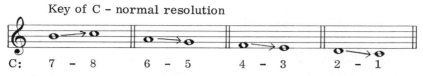

Key of C – normal resolution

C: 7 – 8   6 – 5   4 – 3   2 – 1

Other resolution, determined by approach

C: 7 – 6   6 – 7   4 – 5   2 – 3

Inactive tones within a scale are those which have no strong tendency to move but which create a feeling of repose and completion. These are the tones to which the active tones resolve, and are 1, 3, and 5 in the scale. The third and fifth steps in the scale, while considered inactive, produce a less final sound than the tonic tone in either octave.

Example 4–11.

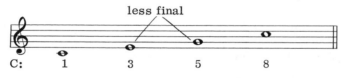

less final

C: 1   3   5   8

SPACING OF NOTES *Melodic Movement*

All melodies are composed of the following classifications of spacing: *Melodies move in one or more of the following ways:*

1. Scale or step.

Example 4–12. KABALEVSKY, Etude, from Op. 27.

2. Skips.

Example 4–13. HINDEMITH, Fugue No. 5, from "Ludus Tonalis."

3. Repeated Notes.

Example 4–14. HAYDN, Variations in f minor.

These three types of motion in a melody seldom occur by themselves, but occur usually in a combination of the three. In the skip type, a triad or other chord will often be used as the basis for the melodic pattern, and in the repeated note type the harmony supporting the melody will often change while the note is repeated in the melody.

MELODIC CONTOUR

There are four basic contours possible in a melody:

1. Ascending melody, starting low and ending high.

Example 4–15. BEETHOVEN, Sonata, Op. 14, No. 2—Scherzo.

2. Descending melody, starting high and ending low.

Example 4–16. MENDELSSOHN, Song Without Words, No. 42.

3. Starting low, ascending, then descending.

Example 4–17. MOZART, Symphony No. 40, in g minor.

4. Starting high, descending, then ascending to a high point.

Example 4–18. HANDEL, Joy to the World.

NOTE: There are many variations of these, as will be observed in the examination of more actual music. Try to make your melodies as beautiful and as interesting as possible, but remember that some of the finest melodies in all music are the simple ones, in many cases those derived from folk music.

METER

This is the plan of the basic accents and note values in a musical composition; it remains constant throughout a composition or until a change is designated. There are two types of meter, simple and compound. *Simple* meter consists of two, three, or four beats to the measure (the numerator in the key signature). $\frac{4}{4}$ time is sometimes indicated by a **C**, which means "common time." *Alla breve,* a tempo mark **¢,** means two half-note beats to the measure or $\frac{2}{2}$, and is sometimes called "cut time." *Compound* meter consists of a simple meter multiplied by three (i.e., $\frac{3}{8}$ is simple meter, $\frac{9}{8}$ is compound meter). There is a third type of meter, *irregular,* which includes those not listed above. Irregular meter is usually a combination of two, three, or four beats forming their own metric pattern. For example, $\frac{5}{8}$ time could be a combination of 3 plus 2, as in the Bartok shown below (Example 4–23), or 2 plus 3. Another possibility is $\frac{7}{4}$ or $\frac{7}{8}$, with a 4-plus-3 combination of beats and accents.

Rhythm consists of the arrangements of notes and rests of different time duration within a framework of a given meter to produce the desired musical effect. *Syncopation,* or the displacement of accents, is in the realm of rhythm, and is often used for interest, as is the dividing of basic beats into smaller segments or the combining of beats.

1. Simple meter.

Example 4–19. CAREY, America.

2. Compound meter.

Example 4–20. CHOPIN, Berceuse, Op. 57.

3. Simple meter with divisions of the beat.

Example 4–21. DOUGLAS MOORE, Fiddlin' Joe.

Copyright © 1936 by Carl Fischer, Inc., New York. Reprinted by permission.

4. Compound meter with syncopation and combining of beats.

Example 4–22. BRAHMS, Romanze, Op. 118, No. 5 (measures 5–8).

5. Irregular meter.

Example 4–23. BARTOK, Bulgarian Rhythm—Mikrokosmos, No. 115.

MOTIVE

The smallest independent fragment of a melody is called a motive, which might be compared to a word or several words in speech. It is composed of at least two notes, has rhythmic implications, and is the germ of musical composition. It is used extensively in the development of a musical idea. Below are two familiar motives:

Example 4–24. GRUBER, Silent Night;   BEETHOVEN, Symphony No. 5.

PHRASE

A phrase *may be* composed of several motives and conveys a single musical idea in much the same way that a phrase conveys an idea in speech. It is the natural division of the musical line. A *period* is also a division of a musical line, but is always a complete musical sentence, being composed of phrases. The usual period contains two phrases and might appear as a question-and-answer type of pattern similar to that found in speech. The first phrase of this type of period is called the "antecedent" and the latter or answer is called the "consequent" phrase. A phrase is often four measures in length, although sometimes it will consist of two, eight, or an irregular number of measures.

If the antecedent and consequent phrases in a period are identical with the exception of the phrase endings, the period is said to have *parallel* construction. If, however, the antecedent and consequent phrases are different in their construction, the period is said to have *contrasting* construction.

Example 4–25.

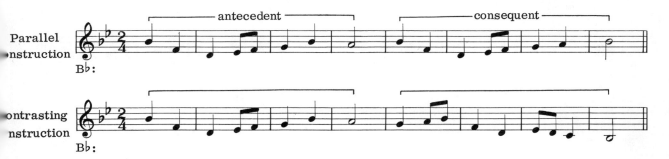

THE MINOR MODE

Melodies in a minor key present a problem in the use of the sixth and seventh scale steps. In writing melodies of a traditional nature, raise the leading tone if the melody does not move *step-wise* from 6 to 7 or from 7 to 6 in the minor scale. If it does move from 6 to 7 or from 7 to 6, use the melodic form of the minor. The best and final test for musical quality in a melody is the ear, and the above suggestions for the sixth and seventh scale steps are simply suggestions. Experiment with various possibilities. Analyze the examples below for an application of this principle.

Example 4–26. Mozart, Sonata in c minor (K457).

Example 4–27. HANDEL, Courante in F.

COMPOSING A MELODY

For the present, use a member of the tonic triad on the first principal accent of the melody. If it begins with an upbeat, use a tone in the V chord for this, which will lead directly to the I on the main accent. In writing a two-phrase period, with antecedent and consequent phrases, end the first (antecedent) phrase with a tone other than the tonic tone and end the consequent phrase with the tonic tone.

Example 4–28.

F: I   V   V   I   V   V   I

Assignments

1. Sing the I, IV, and V triads in any key, with keynote given, as illustrated below.

G: Keynote   I   IV   V

2. When the instructor plays a progression using these three primary triads, sing the above pattern, then say the name of the triad (tonic, etc.). Listen for the difference in the quality of these three chords.

3. Play the I, IV, and V *triads* in any major or minor key, as illustrated below:

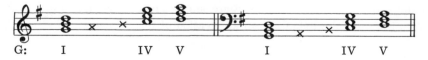

G: I   IV   V   I   IV   V

4. Write four examples of each of the following triads in four-part chorale style in the keys indicated. Use key signatures. In each chord indicate the position of the soprano and label each as to open (O) or close (C) ~~position~~ *spacing*

(a) I in D flat major   (d) V in a minor
(b) iv in c minor   (e) IV in E major
(c) IV in F major   (f) i in g minor

5. Play the I, IV, and V chords in four-part harmony, *piano style,* as illustrated below, with the three upper voices in the right hand in close position, and with the bass note (the root) in the left hand. Play these in all major and minor keys.

6. Write one melody in the key of F major and one in e minor, each one phrase in length and consisting of stepwise motion only. Indicate the contour.

7. Write one melody in the key of G major and one in a minor, each one phrase in length and consisting of motion by skip only. Indicate the contour.

8. Write one melody in the key of D major and one in g minor, each composed of two phrases, combining the types of melodic contour, in compound meter, and with parallel construction.

9. Write a melody in the key of E flat major, two phrases in length with contrasting construction, simple meter, and syncopation. Use the members of the I, IV, and V triads whenever skips occur, and label strategic chords as illustrated in Example 4–28.

10. Write a melody which is free of limitations and describe its structure and nature.

11. In class, analyze melodies of different types in terms of the principles learned in this chapter.

5

HARMONIZATION
IN THE ROOT
POSITION

Basic Principles of Chord Progression

The following factors concerning chord progression represent the strict type of harmonization. Music harmonized by adherence to these principles will be correct and will sound full and complete, but will not be musically satisfying. Once these principles are mastered, a more flexible style will be learned which will be more effective and musical.

VOICE MOVEMENT

Each part should move as smoothly as possible from one chord to another. Exceptions will be made for melodic variety and contrast and for the restricted bass movement.

MELODIC SKIPS

Excessive leaps should be avoided, except when the chord is repeated. In this case the soprano and often the other voices will skip to another chord tone. Skips in the bass part are unavoidable at this point because of chord limitations.

Example 5–1.

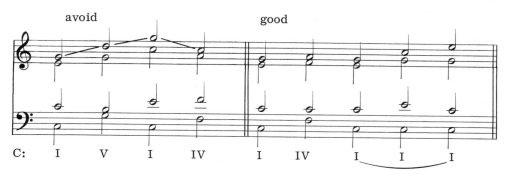

TYPES OF MOTION

Observe the following types of *relative* motion: *between pairs of voices*

1. *Similar*—tones of one interval move in the same direction, but not the same distance.
2. *Parallel*—tones of an interval move the same distance in the same direction.
3. *Contrary*—tones of an interval move in opposite directions.
4. *Oblique*—one tone of an interval remains stationary while the other moves in either direction.

Example 5–2.

PARALLEL FIFTHS AND OCTAVES   *Poor explanation*

No two voices should move in parallel fifths, octaves, or unisons. By parallel fifths we refer to parallel *perfect* fifths. A perfect fifth moving to a diminished fifth, or vice versa, is permissible. Intervals must be moving either up or down in order to be considered parallel; a fifth being repeated, for example, is not a parallel fifth because it is not actually moving. Parallel intervals may occur in any two voices.

The reason for not allowing parallel fifths, octaves, and unisons is that with only four voices at our disposal and the fact that we are writing in the common practice period, the empty, rather hollow quality of these intervals as they move in parallel motion tends to eliminate a voice from the harmonic texture. Also, the effectiveness of each voice is impaired.

Example 5-3.

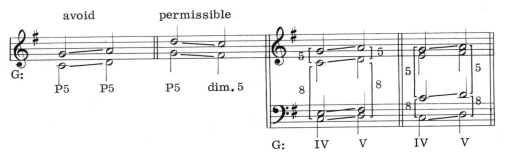

OVERLAPPING

Try to keep the voices clear of each other so that there is no overlapping or crossing of parts. Overlapping often hinders the melodic feeling of the individual voices. One voice should not move beyond an adjacent voice in going to the next chord.

Example 5-4.

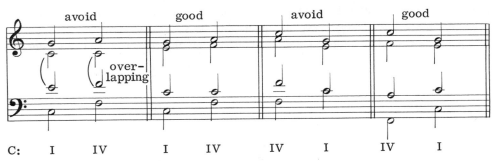

In a more flexible type of harmonization, overlapping is sometimes very effective in highlighting a particular voice or creating a more interesting and freer melodic line. Although we will not adhere to this technique at this time, an observation of a phrase from the following Bach chorale will illustrate this type of voice leading.

Example 5-5. BACH, In allen meinen Taten.

CHORD MOVEMENT *Poor explanation*

Avoid moving all voices in the same direction, if possible. Adherence to this principle contributes to better tonal balance and a stronger feeling of movement within a phrase. Contrary motion of voices, particularly the outer voices, promotes strength and motion. There are two exceptions to this principle. First, in the final progression in a phrase (V to I) all four voices occasionally move down from the V to the final I. Second, this principle does not apply when the first chord is the final chord in a phrase and the second is the first chord of the following phrase. Each phrase is a separate entity.

Example 5–6.

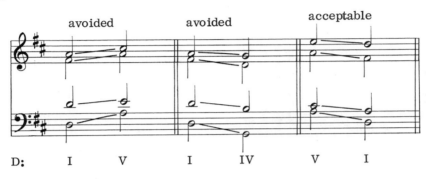

COMPLETE AND INCOMPLETE CHORDS *Poor explanation*

Use complete chords whenever possible, with two roots, a third, and a fifth. Occasionally it will be impossible to use a complete chord in a particular progression because of voice leading, so in this situation give strength to the root and be sure the third is included.

Example 5–7.

CHANGE OF HARMONY

Change the harmony at the beginning of a measure, if possible. This will give a feeling of movement to the phrase and will highlight the principal accent, thus avoiding a flat, static effect.

If a soprano note is repeated, changing the underlying harmony will produce interest as well as intensity.

Connection of I, IV, and V

5th progressions

I–IV–I and I–V–I

1. Construct the first chord.
2. Write the bass (root) of the second chord.
3. Carry over *in the same voice* the tone common to both chords.
4. Lead the two remaining tones of the first chord to the nearest chord tone of the second chord.

Example 5–8.

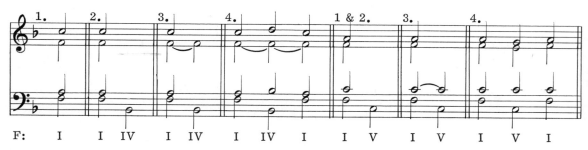

5. Exceptions:
   (a) If no tone can be held over as a common tone because of melodic demands or irregular doubling, lead each of the upper voices to the nearest chord tone, observing the principles of parallel and contrary motion.
   (b) In the progression I–IV, if the bass moves up, the three upper voices may move down to the nearest chord tones. In the progression I–V, if the bass moves down, the upper three voices may move up to the nearest chord tones.

Example 5–9.

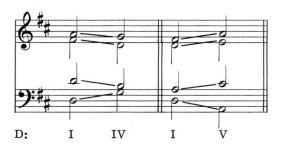

IV–V AND V–IV

1. Construct the first chord.
2. Write the bass of the second chord, moving the bass one step (not a seventh in the opposite direction).

to the nearest tones

3. Lead the upper three voices in contrary motion to the bass, ~~as there is no common tone be-~~ ~~tween these chords.~~

in the 2nd chord

Example 5–10.

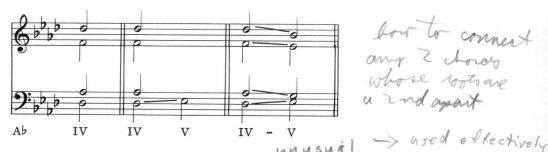

how to connect any 2 chords whose roots are a 2nd apart → *used effectively in Beethoven's 9th*

Ab   IV   IV   V   IV – V

4. The progression V–IV, while occasionally found in music, is ~~rather ineffective~~, because the ear expects the normal resolution of the V to a I or related chord with the leading tone resolving to the tonic tone. If this progression, however, is followed immediately by the V, thus forming V–IV–V, the result is rather effective and may be used.

unusual

Example 5–11.

Bb: V   IV   V   I

Treatment of I, IV, and V in Minor Keys

MINOR RECOGNITION — *Poor – No mention of 3rd*

Before beginning to study a completed work or to harmonize a given bass or soprano, determine whether the mode of the work is major or minor. The most obvious indication of minor is the presence of an accidental representing the raised leading tone and sometimes also the raised sixth step (see "Accidentals" below). The phrase or composition will often begin and conclude with the tonic chord, so these two tones will also determine the mode.

SIXTH AND SEVENTH DEGREES

Chords are connected in the same manner as in major keys.

The augmented second between the sixth and seventh steps of the harmonic minor scale is not normally used melodically. This interval is avoided in the following ways:

1. Lead the sixth scale step down, except in chord repetition.
2. Lead the seventh scale step up to the tonic tone, or, less frequently, move it down a third if it is in an inner voice.

Example 5–12.

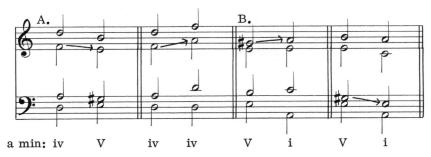

ACCIDENTALS

Be sure the proper accidental is used (raised leading tone) in the V chord, and write this accidental as the chord is written rather than after the phrase is finished. Develop the habit of thinking in minor, of mentally hearing the I and IV chords as minor chords and the V chord as a major chord.

Cadences

In the discussion of the phrase in Chapter 4 (page 44), reference was made to the phrase endings. The conclusion of a phrase, a period, a section, or an entire composition is called a cadence, which serves as the point of destination of all musical ideas. While we will consider the cadence at this time in terms of harmonic progression, the true meaning of the cadence will be revealed only when the melodic and rhythmic aspects of music are considered with the harmonic. Interpretation in performance depends greatly on the understanding of the point of departure, the movement and direction, and finally the conclusion, or point of repose, within each phrase. It is this point of repose that we are concerned with at this time.

There are three basic types of cadences in which the primary triads are used: the authentic, the plagal, and the semi- or half cadence.

AUTHENTIC CADENCE—V–I   awkward

This is the most frequently used cadence in music and the one most often found at the end of a composition. It marks the destination within a musical idea, as was discussed at the beginning of

Chapter 4 where each of the primary triads was discussed. There are two types of authentic cadences, the perfect and the imperfect.

Perfect Authentic Cadence. This is a V–I cadence in which the root is found in both the soprano and bass voices in the final tonic chord. *and the I chord is in root position.*

Example 5–13.

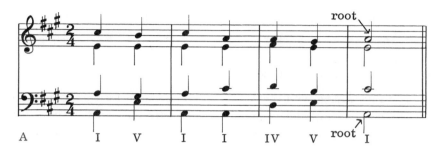

Imperfect Authentic Cadence. This is a V–I cadence having any other arrangement of tones than that found in the perfect authentic cadence. A third or fifth may be in the soprano in the final tonic chord, and/or a note other than the root may be in the bass in the tonic. This is a less final form of the authentic cadence.

Example 5–14.

PLAGAL CADENCE—IV–I

This cadence is sometimes called the "amen" or church cadence, because of its typical use as an "amen" at the end of a hymn. Although it is a final cadence, it does not possess the urgency or the feeling of completion of the authentic cadence, because of the absence of the leading tone in the chord immediately preceding the tonic.

for one reason,

Example 5–15.

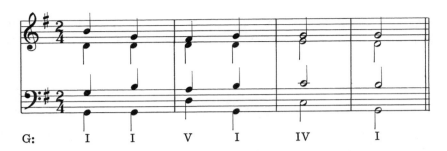

G: I   I   V   I   IV   I

SEMI- OR HALF CADENCE—I–V OR IV–V

This cadence, ~~always~~ usually ending with the V chord, is most often used to complete the antecedent phrase, there being another phrase following which completes the period. This cadence in music is comparable to a comma in speech. Other chords, which will be studied later, may also precede the V chord in a half cadence.

Example 5–16.

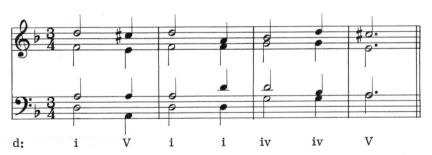

d: i   V   i   i   iv   iv   V

Harmonization of a Given Bass

While the harmonization of a bass part is seldom the procedure in writing music, the discipline and practice in connecting chords, working for variety, and developing good voice leading from a given bass will facilitate the harmonizing of a melody. The following principles will be of value:

1. Apply the principles presented earlier in this chapter for progressions, the bass part being the root of the triad.

2. Lead the upper voices as smoothly as possible when progressing from one chord to a different chord.

3. When the bass note is repeated, change the position of at least two of the upper voices.

4. If a chord is repeated, the bass may skip an octave as long as it remains in the bass range and all voices do not move in the same direction.

5. For melodic and rhythmic interest and for a shift of range, the time value of a bass note may be divided in the upper voices to produce two different arrangements of the same chord.

Example 5–17.

Harmonization of a Given Soprano

Aside from the given principles of harmonization, the sounds of the chords and the understanding of the function of each of the available chords are the most important considerations in the harmonization of a soprano melody. In addition, the music must produce movement toward a goal and must sound well. The following are principles for a soprano harmonization:

1. Determine which available chord or chords may be used to harmonize a given soprano note. Example 5–18 illustrates the available chords for each scale step in the soprano voice.

Example 5–18.

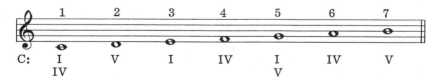

2. Decide which chord, if there is more than one possibility, will best fit the phrase structure and the harmonic scheme desired.

3. If a skip occurs in the soprano part, use the same chord for harmonizing the two notes involved. *Ridiculous*

4. Connect the chords, using the best voice leading possible.

5. If a soprano note is repeated or held, the harmony may be changed for variety.

Example 5-19.

A: I   I   I   V   V   I   IV   V   I   IV   I

Rhythmically unfinished

Free Chorale Style Harmonization

The principles set forth thus far in this chapter represent the basic means of connecting primary chords in the common practice period. By observing these principles one can create a ~~complete-sounding, conservative, and~~ correct piece of music. These will be continually used as our guides. By using exceptions to and adaptations of these principles, we will be able to write music within the four-part framework which *may* ~~will~~ be more interesting ~~and more musical~~. Tread carefully in experimentation with these possibilities. Always keep in mind that the goal is to write something which will sound musically satisfying and which will be convincing horizontally as well as vertically. Experiment with the following possibilities.

COMMON TONE PRINCIPLE

Other kinds of

~~A more musical and stimulating~~ voice leading will be possible if the common tone is not kept in the same voice. In this case be sure that at least one voice is moving in contrary motion to the others. This device should be used only when there would be a definite advantage to such movement and in the case of a given soprano when there is no other alternative.

Example 5-20.

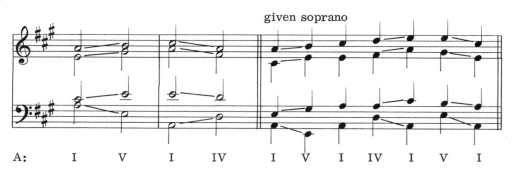

A: I   V   I   IV   I   V   I   IV   I   V   I

DOUBLING

Although the root of the chord is the most satisfactory tone to double, the third or fifth may occasionally be doubled to good advantage. This doubling is used to prevent awkward voice leading or repetition of a single tone in any of the upper voices, and to permit effective scalewise motion. Also, the fifth may be omitted and the root tripled to produce better voice leading. This arrangement often occurs in the I chord at the end of a phrase. Avoid the doubling of the leading tone (the third of the V chord), as it is very active and needs no further emphasis in a progression. *(V.L. & //*
considerations, too.)

Example 5-21.

V.L. = voice leading
// = parallel

3rd doubled   5th doubled   tripled root

A: IV   I   I   IV   V   I   V   I

SOPRANO LINE

Because the soprano and bass voices are the most prominent and create the essence of the phrase, try to create a meaningful contour in the soprano when harmonizing a given bass. The other voices are important, but to a lesser degree than the soprano.

Melody Writing

The next step in the study of original melody writing is that of the harmonic basis of the melody. It is possible to harmonize most simple diatonic melodies with the primary triads. Folk songs, children's songs, and similar works fit this procedure with ease.

CHORDAL FREQUENCY

In the simplest form, one chord may be used to harmonize one or more consecutive measures. A folk tune, having as its harmonic structure one chord per measure, would fit into this type. In Example 5-22, which illustrates this type of melody, the bass notes are written simply to give the chord structure rather than to indicate the principles of voice leading.

Example 5–22. Red River Valley.

In a more involved type the harmony will change with each note in the melody (similar to the four-part writing in this chapter). The following chorale excerpt by Bach illustrates this type of chord frequency.

Example 5–23. BACH, Heut' triumphieret Gottes Sohn.

A third type is a combination of the two described above and is the most frequently used. Here the chord changes are more frequent than in the folk song type and less frequent than in the chorale type.

SKIPS IN A MELODY

Skips often form one of the three primary triads, so the selection of a chord is simplified. Maintain the same harmony, if possible, when these skips occur.

Example 5–24.

SCALE PATTERNS

Sometimes, in a scalewise progression, one may wish to use one chord to harmonize a group of notes in a melody, even if some of these notes do not fit the particular chord. The tones which do not belong to the chord are called "non-harmonic" tones and create interest in the musical line. Although these tones will be studied later, experiment with them now, letting your ear be your guide. In Example 5–25, the non-harmonic tones are designated by a plus (+) sign.

Example 5–25. EMMETT, Dixie.

I, IV, and V in Simple Chord Accompaniment

To accompany singing or to play simple tunes using the I, IV, and V chords, one may use a piano style "chording" technique, alternating the bass note in the left hand with the three-voiced chord in the right hand.

Practice the following patterns with the suggested fingerings in all keys, major and minor. Although the right hand will be in close position, practice these progressions with the soprano in the first measure being first in the position of the fifth, then the third, and finally the octave. These basic patterns can be adapted to fit any chord succession using these chords.

Example 5–26.

Assignments

1. Write the following progressions in four-part harmony, chorale style:

   (a) I–IV–I in G major
   (b) I–V–I in B flat major
   (c) i–iv–i in f sharp minor
   (d) I–IV–I–V–I in E major

   (e) i–V–i in d minor
   (f) I–IV–V–I in C major
   (g) i–iv–V–i in e flat minor
   (h) I–V–IV–V–I in A major

2. As the instructor plays progressions using the I, IV, and V chords, first write the bass part, then the soprano, then determine the chord and write the chord label for each. Indicate the type of cadence.

3. Identify and write the chord labels for progressions of I, IV, and V, as played on the piano by the instructor. Listen for the quality of the chord in the particular key in terms of tendency tones and the relationship of the chord to the tonic tone.

4. Harmonize the following basses in chorale style:

   (a) Strict style.

   (b) Strict style.

   (c) Strict style.

   (d) Free style.

   (e) Free style.

5. Harmonize the following soprano melodies in chorale style:

   (a) Strict style.

(b) Strict style.

(c) Strict style.

(d) Free style.

(e) Free style.

6. Play the progressions I–IV–I, I–V–I, and I–IV–V–I in any major or minor key in piano style, with one note (the bass) in the left hand, and three notes in close position in the right hand. Pianists should experiment with fuller arrangements of these chords, still observing voice leading.

7. Select a folk tune or any simple melody which is well known. Work out a "chording" accompaniment for it and play it with a constant rhythmic pulse as the class sings the song.

8. Write a melody of two phrases in the key of F major with chord labels to suggest the harmonization. End the first phrase with a half cadence and end the second phrase with a perfect authentic cadence.

9. Write an original four-measure exercise in the key of A major, concluding with a plagal cadence.

10. Write an original eight-measure period in the key of E major. End the antecedent phrase with a half cadence and the consequent phrase with an imperfect authentic cadence.

6

THE FIRST
INVERSION

To achieve variety and interest *in the bass line and* in the harmonization of the primary triads, it is possible for these chords to be employed with the third or fifth of the chord, rather than the root, being placed in the bass. In the previous chapters, the root has been in the bass in all chords. The placing of any chord tone other than the root of the chord in the bass voice is called *inversion*. This chapter deals with the *first inversion*, in which the third of the chord is in the bass. The use of inversions demands a more elaborate system of nomenclature of chords and is discussed below.

The Figured Bass

This system of indicating the type of chord or interval to be sounded above a bass note was widely used in the baroque period (1600–1750) and comes down to us as a practical means of indicating specific factors in the chords at our disposal. Frequently, in the baroque period, the composer-conductor-harpsichordist would have before him only the bass part of an orchestral work to be performed, and below this bass would be written figures (numbers) which would indicate the entire harmonic structure. By interpreting these indications, he could amplify the orchestral sound with a full harmonic background or could emphasize what he wished. This system is also called *thorough-bass* or *basso continuo* and was used for instructional purposes as well as for performing with a group.

Example 6–1. BACH, B minor Mass, No. 51 (*organo e continuo*).

We now use the figured bass as a means of facilitating the study of chord structure and movement, but we dispense with its use in free composition, once the knowledge of chords and chord progression is mastered. Learn the following essential facts regarding the figured bass.

ARABIC NUMERALS

The numerals, either alone or following the Roman numeral (chord label) below the bass note, indicate the corresponding interval to be found in the chord constructed above this bass note in the key designated by the key signature. For example, if a 6 appears after the Roman numeral I, and the bass note is E in the key of C major, you would find C in an upper voice, as a sixth above E is C.

Example 6–2.

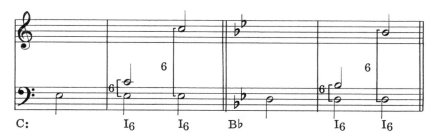

THIRDS, FIFTHS, AND OCTAVES

These intervals are not normally indicated in the figured bass but are understood, unless they *in root position* represent notes which are essential to the analysis of the particular chord. A tonic chord would be completely figured as I_3^8, but we simplify this to I, because the numbers are understood. Therefore, a bass note without a number following the Roman numeral indicates a triad in root position. *Or a bass note without number or Roman numeral indicates a triad in root position.*

Example 6–3.

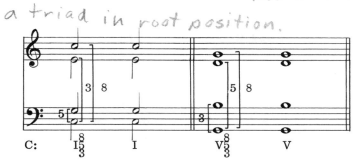

ACCIDENTALS

The accidentals to be found in the chord are indicated by a sharp, flat, or natural sign placed after the number indicating the interval to be altered. An accidental appearing by itself with no number to qualify it indicates that the *third* above this bass note is so affected. Sometimes a diagonal line is drawn through the number instead of using an accidental, to indicate that the interval in question is to be raised.

Example 6–4.

CONSECUTIVE NUMBERS

Two or more consecutive numbers indicate the movement of one upper voice using these tones; this does not affect the structure of the entire chord. A dash following a number indicates that the note involved is to be held in the same voice.

(intervals indicate above bass)

Example 6–5. BACH, Aus meines Herzens Grunde.

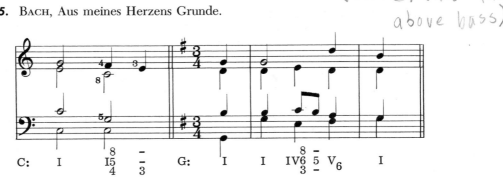

First Inversion of Triads

STRUCTURE

The third of a first inversion chord is located in the bass, and the root and fifth are found a sixth and a third above the bass, respectively. Therefore, the complete figured bass symbol for a first inversion triad would be $\frac{6}{3}$. The number 3 is omitted from this figured bass symbol because it is understood, so the symbols for the primary triads in the first inversion are I_6, IV_6, and V_6. This symbol applies to all other triads in the first inversion as well.

Example 6–6.

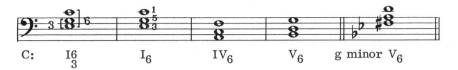

QUALITY AND FUNCTION

The identity of a triad is not destroyed by inverting it, but the stability and function within a progression are altered with its use. The "six-chord," as it is sometimes called, is less emphatic and less basic than the same chord in root position. It is lighter in texture, whereas the root position chord is more solid. A six-chord may be used as a substitute for or in addition to the same chord in root position. It should not be used to complete a phrase or composition in four-part writing, strict or free. The principal functions of the six-chord are to provide a contrast in texture and to create a more musical and interesting bass line than is possible with root position chords exclusively.

Note in Example 6–7 how the six-chords stimulate movement and create a more musical bass line. Although the soprano is the same in both phrases, the texture is altered in the second phrase.

Example 6–7.

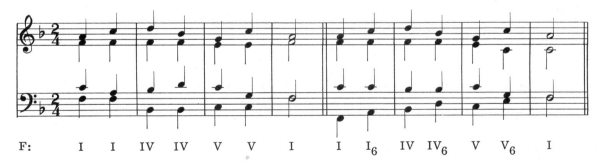

DOUBLING

No chord requires as much care and good judgment in its use as the six-chord. This is due to the problem of doubling. In any chord, those tones are usually doubled which contribute most to the solidity of the key. In the case of the primary six-chords the *root or fifth* is normally doubled, *not* the third, which is the bass note.

Voice leading in all voices and the melodic feeling of the soprano line will be the determining factors in deciding which of the two, the root or the fifth, should be doubled. The third may be doubled in the I_6 or IV_6 chords only if better voice leading will result by means of stepwise or contrary motion. The V_6 chord rarely appears with a doubled third, because this third is the leading tone and to double it would make the chord unbalanced in sound.

Example 6–8.

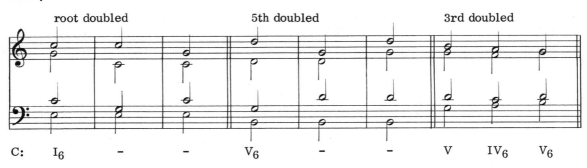

SIX-CHORDS IN PROGRESSION

In general, the principles of voice leading and chord progression are the same for six-chords as for chords in root position. The points below refer specifically to I_6, IV_6, and V_6.

1. When there is more than one common tone between six-chords or between root position chords and six-chords, observe the common tone principle in at least one voice. The other voice or voices may skip or move by step. The soprano voice should have more freedom of movement than the other voices.

Example 6–9.

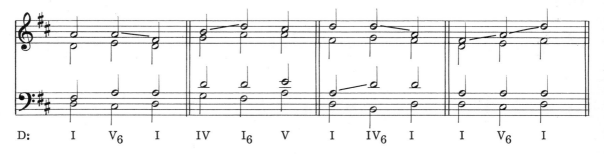

2. A root position chord may be followed by its first inversion for relief and variety in the bass. Less often and less effectively the six-chord may be followed by the chord in root position, as it does little to stimulate motion in the phrase. (See also Example 6–7.) *Question of relations of chord "weight" and metric accent is also involved.*

Example 6–10.

3. Irregardless of our attempts to create a smooth bass line when using these six-chords, the bass may skip a sixth or an octave effectively and may also move an augmented fourth or a diminished fifth to the leading tone.

Example 6–11.

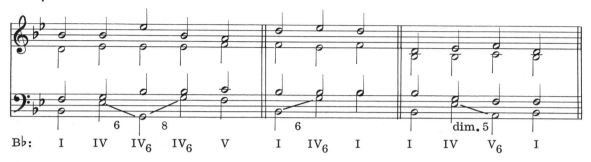

4. These chords are effectively used in succession; a good feeling of movement results. The possibility of parallel fifths and octaves is great in such a progression, so alternate doublings and contrary motion are recommended for good balance and voice leading.

Example 6–12.

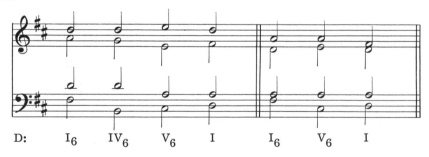

5. The IV$_6$ may either precede or follow V. In these progressions the roots of the two chords in question move in contrary motion to the other voices, but are now located in one of the upper voices.

Example 6–13.

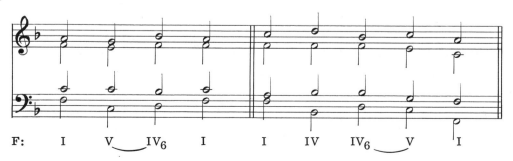

SOPRANO HARMONIZATION

Use the procedures presented in Chapter 5 in harmonizing a given soprano. Add to the table listed in Example 5–18 (page 55) the following chord possibilities. Until you learn the harmonic possibilities for each scale step in the soprano voice, it might be wise to keep a table such as the one below in a separate place in your notebook and add to it as new possibilities are presented.

Example 6–14.

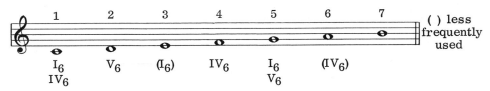

Melody Writing—Simple Binary Form

Simple *binary* or *two-part* form consists of two balanced phrases or sections. It is often called "AB" form and strongly resembles the musical sentence or period discussed on page 43, except that now it has been enlarged or extended.

The melodic and harmonic structure of the first section is basically different from that of the second section, although rhythmically it may be very similar. The length of each section may vary, from 8 or 16 measures in the simple works to many more measures in the more complex works. Examples of music in this form can be found in all styles and periods, the differences between one and another being the extent of complexity, the medium for which the music was written, and the general style of composition.

Example 6–15 illustrates a familiar song in AB form, the first section of six measures and the second section of eight measures both ending with a perfect authentic cadence. Note the difference in contour of the two sections and the similarity of the rhythmic patterns in the first four measures of each section. Despite the individuality of each section, the mood and basic plan of the entire work are obvious.

Example 6–15. CAREY, America.

Example 6–16 is another familiar song, but here each of the two sections consists of eight measures. The first section ends with a half cadence and the second section ends with a perfect authentic cadence. The half cadence is a temporary point of rest suggesting a modulation or change of key, which heightens the interest and demands movement.

Example 6–16. KUCKEN, How Can I Leave Thee.

Non-harmonic Tones—The Passing Tone

Non-harmonic tones are those which are foreign to the chords which they embellish. They add interest, *make possible a more conjunct melodic line* ~~develop a better melodic feeling~~, and add color to a harmonic progression. They may occur in any voice with good effect, but they are found most frequently in the soprano voice. They may occur separately or in combination, and when in combination may be used either in parallel or contrary motion. There are two basic types of non-harmonic tones, the *accented* and the *unaccented*, and the characteristics of each of the special kinds of non-harmonic tones studied will be determined to a certain extent by whether it is accented or unaccented.

NOTE: Because of the great discrepancy in terminology and definition of non-harmonic terms by theorists, the terminology most generally accepted will be used here. Attention, however, will be directed to some of the other interpretations as well. It is more important to understand and know how to use a particular non-harmonic tone than to argue about its name.

The passing tone is a non-harmonic tone which is approached and left stepwise in the same direction. There are two types of passing tones, the *unaccented* and the *accented*.

THE UNACCENTED PASSING TONE

This form, which is more generally used, occurs on the unaccented (weak) part of the beat and is not sounded on the accent or with a chord, but rather between two chords. There may be one or more passing tones in succession, depending upon the interval existing between the two chords in one voice. Also, the passing tone may be diatonic or chromatic, depending upon the effect desired. Example 6–17 is a simple, four-part harmonization followed by the same progression with passing tones added. The unaccented passing tone is indicated by P.

Example 6–17.

Example 6–18 shows the use of unaccented passing tones in a chorale excerpt.

Example 6–18. BACH, Nun danket alle Gott.

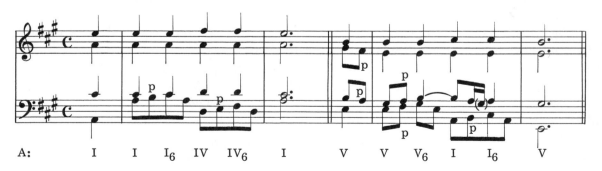

THE ACCENTED PASSING TONE

This is sounded with the chord which may or may not be on an accented beat, but the passing tone is still approached and left stepwise in the same direction. This creates more tension and interest than the unaccented passing tone, because of the dissonance momentarily produced. The resolution of the accented passing tone is the delayed chord tone and is used to determine the chord structure. This passing tone is indicated by an AP.

"Note of resolution" — whether in passing or accented passing tone does not usually appear in another voice unless at an interval of octave or more from note of resolution

Example 6–19.

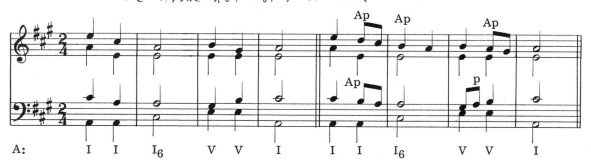

Example 6–20. Mozart, Sonata (K281) (*Andante amoroso*).

Keyboard Work Using I₆, IV₆, and V₆

In piano style using six-chords, again play three notes in the right hand and one, the *bass* note, in the left hand. With the exception of these inverted chords, close position will still be observed in the right hand.

In playing these six-chords, two facts will be apparent:

1. In doubling the root or fifth, the right hand will either encompass an octave or will play only two notes, the root or fifth. In doubling the third, which is less common, the triad will be played by the right hand.
2. When the root or fifth is doubled, you will find the third in the bass but not in the upper voices.

Example 6–21.

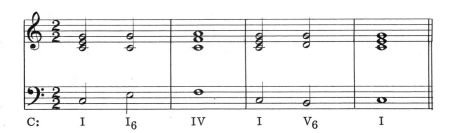

Play different rhythmic patterns with these progressions, as illustrated in Chapter 5.

Assignments

1. Write the following progressions in four parts, chorale style:

   (a) I–I$_6$–IV–I in A major
   (b) i–V$_6$–i in b minor
   (c) i$_6$–iv–V–i in c sharp minor
   (d) i$_6$–iv$_6$–V$_6$–i in f sharp minor

   (e) i–iv$_6$–V–i in g minor
   (f) I–V–IV$_6$–I in D flat major
   (g) I–V–V$_6$–V$_6$–I in E flat major
   (h) i–iv–i$_6$–V–i in f minor

2. As the instructor plays progressions using the I, IV, and V chords and their first inversions, first write the bass part, then the soprano then determine the precise chord (root position or inversion) and write the chord label for each. Indicate the type of cadence.

3. Identify and write the chord labels for progressions of I, IV, and V and their first inversions, as played by the instructor. By listening carefully to the bass and the quality of the chord, learn to distinguish between the root position chord and its first inversion.

4. Play the progressions which appear in the keyboard work section in all major and minor keys. Non-pianists: Play these in blocked chord formation, as in the second example, but maintaining a steady pulse. Pianists: Play these with different types of rhythmic chording patterns.

5. Harmonize the following basses, using passing tones. Label all chords and label the unaccented passing tones with P and the accented passing tones with AP. Maintain stability, but work for variety and musical sense in writing. Use passing tones only where they will contribute to the musical quality of the exercise.

   (a)

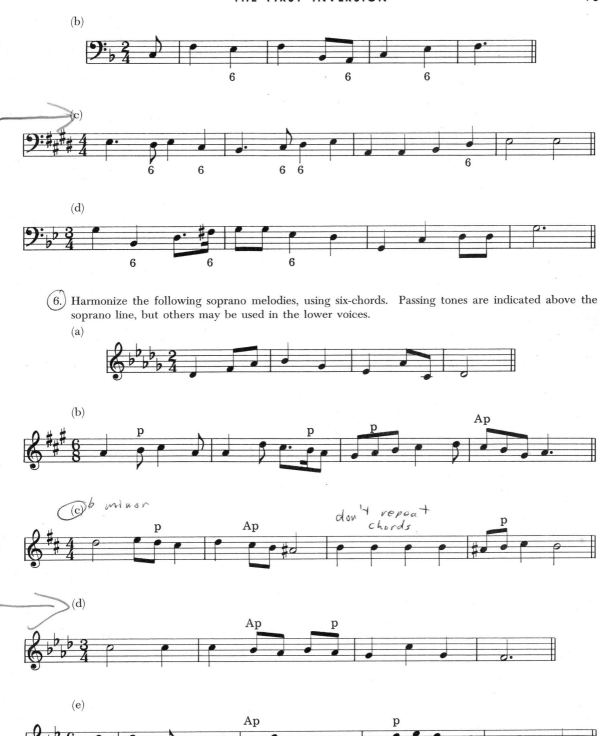

6. Harmonize the following soprano melodies, using six-chords. Passing tones are indicated above the soprano line, but others may be used in the lower voices.

7. Write one original exercise in major and one in minor, each including six-chords and passing tones. These must be at least eight measures in length and may be in any key other than C major and a minor.

8. Experiment with free writing by adapting one of the completed exercises in the preceding assignment to a non-chorale style. Alter the rhythm, repeat chords, create a work from this basic skeleton for piano, for instrument with accompaniment, or for any other medium. The basic harmonic structure must remain, but any standard composition may be used as a model of style.

9. Write a melody in AB form, concluding part A with a half cadence and part B with a perfect authentic cadence. Write chord labels below the melody to suggest a possible harmonization and include six-chords in this skeleton structure. Use passing tones in the melody to achieve a more musical feeling.

10. At the piano, work out the basic harmony for "Lullaby," by Brahms, or the tune worked out in assignment 6 of Chapter 5. Play a rhythmic chording accompaniment to this, using six-chords, as the class sings the melody.

11. Analyze the following excerpts. Determine the chord structure, study and discuss the application of principles of harmonic progression learned to date, analyze the melody, determine the type of cadence, and discuss the style of writing.

(a) O Come, All Ye Faithful.

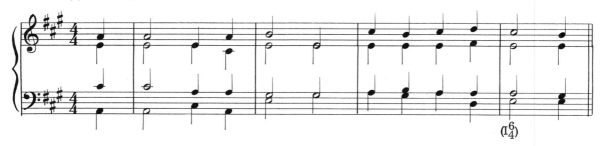

(b) MUIR, The Maple Leaf Forever.

(c) KIRNBERGER, Menuet.

(d) Mozart, Sonata (K332) (*Adagio*).

12. In a similar manner, analyze, bring to class, and discuss music which you are studying which illustrates the primary triads in root position and in first inversion and passing tones.

7

THE $\frac{6}{4}$ CHORD

Because the use of triads in the second inversion is limited basically to the primary triads, this part of the study will be presented now, with applications to other triads later. Although, in a sense, the second inversion triads are not independent chords at all, they are considered here because of their specific functions rather than because of their limitations.

STRUCTURE

In the second inversion of a triad the fifth of the chord is located in the bass voice, the two remaining tones of the triad being located a sixth and a fourth above the bass. This inversion is labeled $\frac{6}{4}$.

Example 7–1.

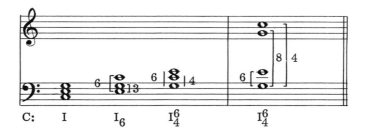

QUALITY AND FUNCTION

The six-four chord lacks the strong feeling of independence which is found in the same chord in root position. This chord is not harmonically essential, but, when placed between two chords with more stability or immediately before a chord which it serves, it tends to expand or extend the existing harmonic progression or heighten the effectiveness of the chord of resolution. In music of the common practice period, the six-four chord is an active, dependent chord which demands movement into a logical chord of resolution. It may be analyzed as the chord of resolution with non-harmonic tones.

Example 7–2. MOZART, Sonata (K332) (*Allegro*).

DOUBLING

The bass note in a six-four chord is doubled. This is the fifth of the chord and this note plus the other fifth which is doubled normally remain stationary in the customary resolution of this chord. This type of voice movement contributes to the lack of independence of the six-four chord. Exceptions to the doubling of the bass note are rare, although on occasion the root of the chord may be doubled for a particular effect. For the present, however, double the bass only.

Example 7–3.

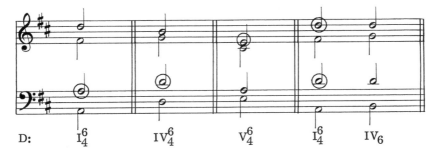

Tonic Six-Four

CADENTIAL SIX-FOUR

Certainly the most successful and most frequently used six-four chord is the I_4^6 which immediately precedes the V in a half or authentic cadence—thus the name, "cadential six-four." It usually occurs on an accented beat with the V following on the unaccented beat. The effect of the combination of these two chords is, in a sense, that of one sound, the V, with the two moving voices serving as non-harmonic tones. Because the I_4^6 is placed immediately before the V in a cadence and anticipates it, the logical chords of preparation are those which most naturally precede the V, for now these are the I and IV.

Example 7–4.

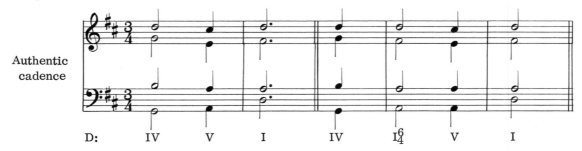

Authentic
cadence

D: IV   V   I   IV I_4^6 V   I

The I_4^6 resolves into the V as smoothly as possible, the bass and the note doubling it remaining stationary and the other two notes moving down stepwise. The bass may skip an octave for a stronger feeling rather than remain stationary, but the effect of the bass voice will still be that of V.

Example 7–5.

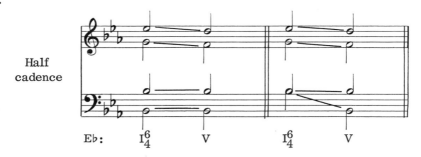

Half
cadence

E♭: I_4^6 V I_4^6 V

EXTENSION OF THE TONIC CHORD

The I_4^6 chord may be used in the repetition of the tonic harmony as simply another arrangement or extension of I for variety. The other six-four chords may be used in the same capacity.

Example 7–6.

F: I I_6 I_4^6 IV   V   I

PASSING CHORD AND NEIGHBORING CHORD

This chord may be used as a passing chord, appearing between IV and IV₆ as an extension of the IV harmony, or as a neighboring chord (the neighboring tone is discussed later in this chapter) in which it serves as an elaboration of the V harmony.

Example 7–7.

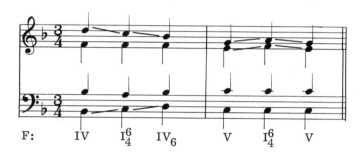

F: IV I$_4^6$ IV₆ V I$_4^6$ V

INDEPENDENT CHORD

A less effective use may be made of the I$_4^6$ chord early in the phrase, resolving to a form of V or another logical resolution of the I harmony, but not in a cadential manner. The six-four chord here will usually appear on an unaccented part of the measure.

Example 7–8.

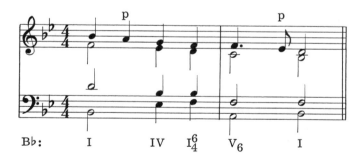

B♭: I IV I$_4^6$ V₆ I

Subdominant Six-Four

This chord, usually occurring in the unaccented part of a measure, is sometimes called an *embellishing six-four*, because its normal function is that of connecting two basic chords by the use of neighboring or passing tones. It is usually supported on either side by I, although it may be preceded by IV, and it tends to expand the tonic harmony, either during a phrase or in a plagal cadence. If the IV$_4^6$ is used too much, the bass part will lack momentum and the result will be one of monotony.

Example 7–9.

A: I   IV$_4^6$ I   I   IV$_4^6$ I   I   IV$_4^6$ I   IV IV$_4^6$ I

Dominant Six-Four

Similar to the IV$_4^6$, this chord also occurs on the unaccented part of the measure and is referred to as a *passing six-four*, because its principal function is that of connecting I with I$_6$ by means of a passing chord. This passing chord is harmonically non-essential, but it promotes smoothness of line.

Example 7–10.

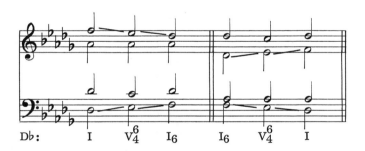

Db: I   V$_4^6$ I$_6$ I$_6$ V$_4^6$ I

Soprano Harmonization of Six-Four Chords

Use the principles presented in previous chapters for harmonizing a given soprano and add to the soprano chord selection table the following possibilities involving six-four chords. Note that each six-four chord and its root position chord may be used to harmonize the same soprano note.

Example 7–11.

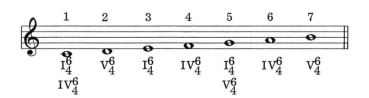

Melody Writing—Ternary Form

This form, also called the *A B A* or *three-part song form*, consists of three separate parts, each being complete in itself, with the third part being a repetition of the first. It is the most widely used form in music because of the feeling of balance and symmetry it produces. It was the form used for the eighteenth-century *"da-capo"* aria, for the combining of two classical dances, and it constitutes the structural form of many of the popular tunes of our own time.

The first or main section (A) is followed by a contrasting section of new material (B), which is often in a related key. This is followed by a return to the original material (A), creating the balance, mentioned above. Part A is frequently repeated before part B is presented, the repetition being identical or with slight variations for interest. The result is A A B A, the most widely used version of the A B A form.

Example 7–12. FRENCH FOLK SONG, Au clair de la lune.

The Neighboring Tone

The neighboring tone is a non-harmonic tone which appears between a chord tone and its repetition. The harmony may change, but the neighboring tone must return to the original tone. Although it is usually unaccented, it appears as an accented neighboring tone on rare occasions. As to its structure, the neighboring tone is approached and left by a step, either up or down. It may move a scale step, half or whole, or it may move chromatically. It may be used singly or in pairs and may occur in any voice or voices, although it is found most frequently in the soprano voice. The neighboring tone is sometimes referred to as a "changing tone," an "auxiliary tone," or an "alternating tone." The neighboring tone is indicated by N.

In the Bach illustration (Example 7–13), there appears a double neighboring tone in the treble in the second measure in which each of the voices moves a half step, then returns to the original note. In the bass voice of the same measure is found a combination of neighboring tones and passing tones employing the raised sixth and seventh steps of the ascending melodic minor scale. In the Beethoven illustration (Example 7–14), the double passing tones are important elements of the melodic line and build tension to the E natural and G natural in the second measure. Listen to these two excerpts with and without the neighboring tones to point up the effectiveness of these tones.

Example 7–13.   BACH, *Polonaise.*

Example 7–14.   BEETHOVEN, *Sonata, Op. 14, No. 2 (Allegro).*

Keyboard Work Using Six-Four Chords

In piano style using six-four chords, play the complete triad in any of the three soprano positions with the right hand and play the fifth of the chord in the left hand. Make sure to resolve the chord properly by moving the necessary voices as little as possible.

Example 7–15.

Assignments

1. Write the following progressions in four parts, chorale style:

   (a) I–IV–I$_4^6$–V–I in G major   (d) I–IV$_6$–I$_4^6$–IV–I in B major
   (b) i–iv$_4^6$–i–V$_6$–i in d minor   (e) IV–V–I$_4^6$–V–I in E flat major
   (c) i–V$_4^6$–i$_6$–iv–V–V$_6$–i in f minor   (f) i–i$_6$–iv–iv$_4^6$–i in c sharp minor

2. As the instructor plays progressions using the I, IV, and V chords and their first and second inversions, write the bass voice and the soprano, then determine the precise chord from the bass and soprano and from the sound of the chord. Write the chord label for each.

3. Identify and write the chord labels for progressions of the chords studied thus far, as played by the instructor.

4. Play the progression which appears in the keyboard work section in all major and minor keys. Non-pianists: Play these as illustrated with a steady pulse. Pianists: Play them as illustrated but add passing tones and neighboring tones where desirable.

5. Harmonize the following basses, using passing tones and neighboring tones. Label all chords and passing tones and label the neighboring tones with "N."

   (a)

(b)

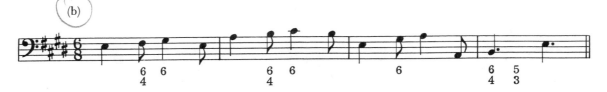

(c) Unfigured bass.

6. Harmonize the following soprano melodies, using root position chords, six-chords, and six-four chords. Passing tones and neighboring tones are indicated above the soprano line but others may be used in the lower voices.

(a)

(b)

(c)

(d)

(e)

7. Play the following cadences in all major and minor keys in keyboard style:

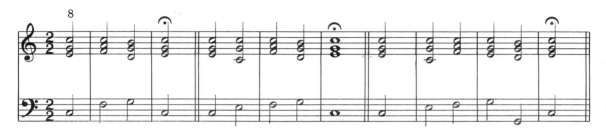

8. Create progressions using the various types of six-four chords as directed by the instructor. Play these in keyboard style without writing them first.

9. Sing major and minor triads in the six-four position from a given note or in a suggested key as illustrated:

Major

10. Write one original exercise in major and one in minor, each including six-chords, six-four chords, passing tones, and neighboring tones. These must be at least eight measures in length.

11. Adapt one of the completed exercises in the preceding assignment to a non-chorale style. It may be for voices, instruments, or piano, and may be written for fewer or more than four parts.

12. Write a free original composition in A B A form, using the harmonic materials studied thus far and also experimenting with other chords. Each section should be either four or eight measures in length. It may be written in any medium. Write this with expression markings, dynamics indications, and tempo indications; perform it in class.

13. Analyze the following excerpts in the same manner as in Chapter 6, giving special attention to six-four chords and neighboring tones.

(a) BACH, Jesu, nun sei gepreiset (final phrase).

(b) MOZART, Sonata (K309) (*Rondo*).

(c) Schumann, Wild Horseman, Op. 68, No. 8.

(d) Mozart, Variations on "Wilhelm von Nassau" (from var. 4).

14. In a similar manner, analyze, bring to class, and discuss music being studied which illustrates the material in this chapter.

8

THE DOMINANT
SEVENTH

One of the most widely used chords in all music, and particularly in the common practice period, is the dominant seventh chord. We have learned that the dominant is perhaps the most important chord in music and now will become familiar with the dominant seventh chord, its most useful version. The study of this chord will be undertaken at this point rather than after that of the II, III, VI, and VII chords, because of its frequent occurrence and importance.

STRUCTURE

By adding the interval of a third to any triad, a seventh chord is formed. The structure of the dominant seventh chord is that of a major triad and a minor seventh and this remains the same in major or in minor because the dominant triad is major in both modes. This form of the seventh chord is found only on the dominant of the key. In our study, the dominant seventh chord represents the first use of four different chord tones in four-part harmony. Seventh chords built on the other scale degrees have a different structure and are not as frequently used. These will be discussed in a separate chapter.

The complete chord label for the dominant seventh chord is $V_{5\atop3}^{7}$, but we will use V_7, as the other numerals are understood.

Example 8-1.

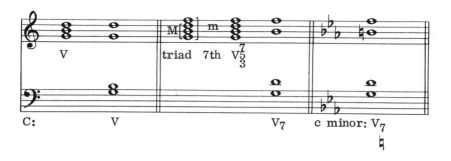

HISTORICAL DEVELOPMENT

The V_7 began as a dominant chord with an added seventh appearing as a passing tone between the doubled upper root of the V and a chord tone in the following chord. It also appeared in the role of a neighboring tone. In the example below by William Byrd (1542–1623) note the D in the alto part at the end of measure 3 in which the seventh of the V_7 appears on the final eighth of the measure and resolves to the C sharp, a raised third in a final tonic in a minor key. The tenor part at the end of the second measure is an added seventh to the V chord which dominated the entire measure. In this case the seventh serves as a neighboring tone, returning to the E in the next measure.

Example 8-2. BYRD, Pavane, The Earle of Salisbury.

In the Bach excerpt (Ex. 8–3), the treatment of the seventh in the next to the final chord, while melodic, is now a chord tone and produces the dissonant effect of a seventh sounding with the triad. Both of these treatments of the seventh of the chord have been in constant usage up to our own time.

Example 8–3. BACH, Wachet auf, ruft uns die Stimme.

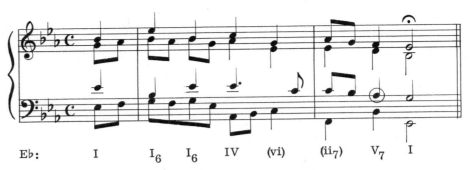

Eb: I   I₆   I₆   IV   (vi)   (ii₇)   V₇   I

CHARACTERISTICS

The V_7 unmistakably clarifies and reveals the tonality, much more so than does the V triad. It is used in place of or in addition to the V chord where more color and intensity are desired. Because it includes the leading tone, the V chord has an urgency to resolve, but with the seventh added there is a still greater magnetic pull to the chord of resolution. The V_7 may be used as a substitute for the V chord in most cases, except in a half cadence, where the V is preferred. Here a temporary point of repose is desired with no strong feeling of resolution being demanded. Because it has more color and forward drive than the V chord, the V_7 should not be used as a substitute for every V chord, because then the effect of the V_7 would be lessened. Good taste and a feeling of balance will determine its frequency.

Example 8–4.

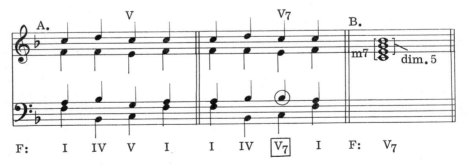

F: I   IV   V   I   I   IV   V₇   I   F: V₇

The most important factors in the V_7 chord are the two dissonant intervals, the *minor seventh* from the root to the seventh and the *diminished fifth* from the third of the chord to the seventh (see illustration B in Example 8–4). These give a feeling of pressure and demand resolution more forcefully than do the intervals in the V triad.

DOUBLING

In four-part harmony the V_7 chord appears most frequently as a complete chord, with all four tones present. Thus there is no need for doubling when the chord is complete. When it appears as an incomplete seventh chord, however, the fifth is omitted and the root doubled. The incomplete V_7 chord is as effective as the complete V_7 chord, because the characteristic intervals of the minor seventh and the diminished fifth are still present.

Example 8–5.

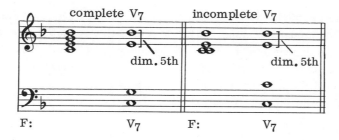

HARMONIC APPROACH

Any chord may precede the V_7 which normally precedes the V, and the V may precede its own V_7. The voice leading will be basically the same as that of the V, but the seventh of the chord is the one tone which needs special consideration. The seventh of the chord may be approached in three ways: (a) it may be prepared, that is, carried over from the same tone in the preceding chord; (b) it may be approached by a step, or (c) it may be approached by a skip. The smoothest and most unobtrusive approach is by preparation, but the approaches by step and by skip are progressively more striking and call more attention to the seventh of the chord.

Example 8–6.

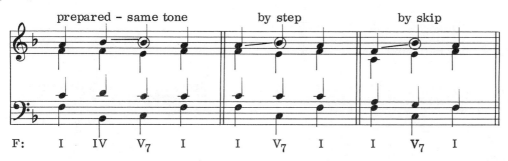

RESOLUTION

The principal consideration here is the resolution of the diminished fifth interval within the V_7 chord. The normal resolution of the diminished fifth in major keys is to a major third, and if the diminished fifth is inverted, the resulting augmented fourth will resolve to a minor sixth. In minor keys the diminished fifth resolves to a minor third and the augmented fourth formed by the inversion resolves to a major sixth. This represents the most natural inclination of the two most active degrees in the scale.

Example 8–7.

C: dim. 5   M3   Aug. 4   m6   c min: dim. 5   m3   Aug. 4   M6

The normal resolution of the V_7 is to the I, one of the most basic progressions in music and the ultimate goal of all traditional harmonic progressions. In this resolution the seventh of the chord resolves down one scale degree into the third of the following I chord. The third of the V_7 chord (the lower factor in the diminished fifth interval) resolves up to the root of the I, the root of the V_7 chord goes to the root of the I, and the fifth of the V_7 resolves down one scale degree to the root of the I, thus resulting in an incomplete I with three roots and one third.

Example 8–8.

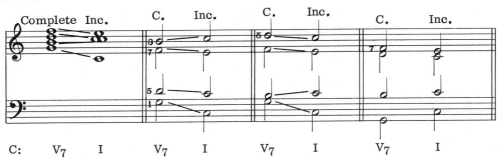

C: V_7 I V_7 I V_7 I V_7 I

Example 8–9. BEETHOVEN, Sonata, Op. 49, No. 1 (*Allegro*) (measures 5–8).

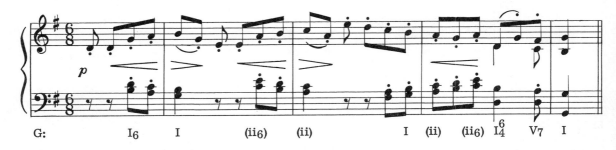

G: I_6 I   (ii$_6$)   (ii)   I   (ii)   (ii$_6$) I$_4^6$ V_7 I

If the V_7 is incomplete, consisting of two roots, a third, and a seventh, the third, seventh, and root (in the bass) move as above, but the doubled root in an upper voice remains on the same tone to become the fifth of the resulting I chord. This I chord of resolution is complete.

Therefore, if the V_7 is complete, the resulting I will be incomplete, and if the V_7 is incomplete, the resulting I will be complete.

Example 8–10.

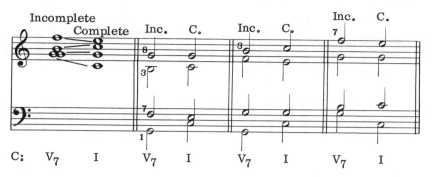

Example 8–11. BEETHOVEN, Sonata, Op. 27, No. 2 (*Allegretto*).

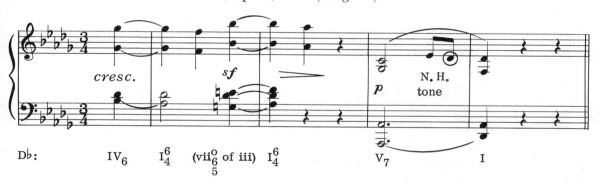

If the third of the V_7 (the leading tone) is in an inner voice in the complete V_7 chord, it may descend the interval of a third to the fifth of the resulting I chord, thus making both the V_7 and the I resolution complete chords. In this progression all voices may move down with good effect, especially at the end of a phrase. The irregular voice leading of the leading tone is possible here because, although the alto and tenor voices are melodic, the downward drop of the leading tone is not as noticeable as it would be in the soprano voice which normally carries the melody.

Example 8–12.

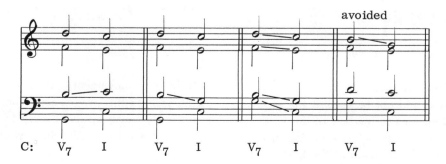

Example 8–13. Beethoven, Sonata, Op. 2, No. 3 (*Allegro con brio*).

C: I   (embellishments) V – V_7 (embellishments) I –

On rare occasions one finds an example of a V_7 in which the third is omitted and the fifth is present in an incomplete V_7 chord. This does not produce the full sound of the V_7, because the characteristic sound of the diminished fifth is absent. This structure may be used, however, where lightness of texture and intensity is desired.

Example 8–14.

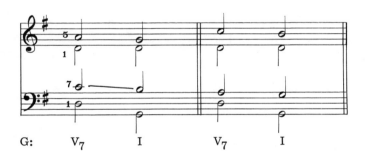

G: V_7 I V_7 I

Example 8–15. Haydn, Sonata in e minor (*Adagio*).

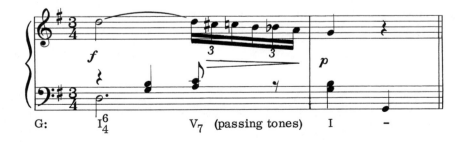

G: I_4^6 V_7 (passing tones)   I   –

The V_7 may resolve to a I_6 in order to achieve a feeling of movement and lightness within a phrase. This should not be used at the conclusion of a phrase. In this progression, where the third of the chord appears in the bass of the I_6, the seventh of the V_7 moves up one degree to the fifth of the I chord to provide better doubling in the I_6. The irregular voice leading here is effective because of the non-basic sound of the I_6 chord.

Example 8-16.

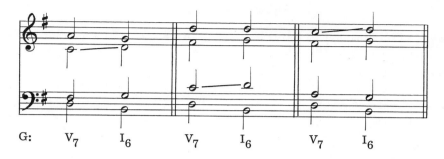

Another irregular voice leading results in a I chord with doubled thirds. In this instance the fifth of the V_7 moves up a step to the third of the I chord. The diminished fifth resolves as usual, although the leading tone (third of the V_7) may drop a third to the fifth of the I chord. This progression is used for melodic freedom primarily and produces a lighter texture while still retaining the I in root position.

Example 8-17.

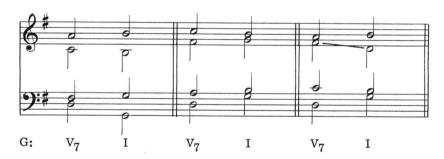

Example 8-18. HAYDN, Sonata in E flat—Finale *(presto)*.

Inversions of V₇

It has been observed that inversions tend to create more possibilities for interest and variety than the same chords in root position. This is even more apparent when considering the V_7 chord, because, with four different tones at our disposal, three inversions are now possible instead of the two inversions of triads. As was true of the inversions of triads, the first inversion is formed with the chord-third in the bass, the second inversion with the chord-fifth in the bass. Now the third inversion is added with the chord-seventh in the bass. Tones are rarely omitted from the inversions of V_7, but these exceptions will be discussed with the particular inversion involved. The root of the chord, now in an upper voice, is normally carried over as a common tone to the fifth of the I resolution.

An easy way to remember the figured bass numerals is to recognize the logical order of the numerals from the root position down.

Example 8–19.

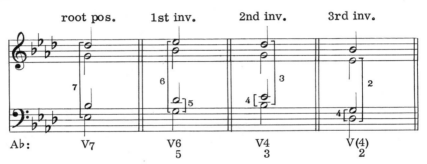

FIRST INVERSION

In the V_5^6 chord, the leading tone is found in the bass voice, which produces a smooth melodic line for the bass from the leading tone to the tonic. This chord has a lighter texture than the V_7. The voices move in the same manner as in root position, except for the root, which remains stationary. The normal resolution is to I.

Example 8–20.

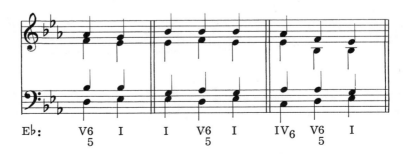

Example 8–21. BEETHOVEN, Sonata, Op. 7 (*Allegro*).

An incomplete V_5^6, with the fifth omitted and the root doubled, will create interest by resolving to a I chord with either a doubled fifth (the doubled root of the V_5^6 carrying over the common tone) or a doubled root (the root of the V_5^6 skipping an interval of a fourth or fifth).

Example 8–22.

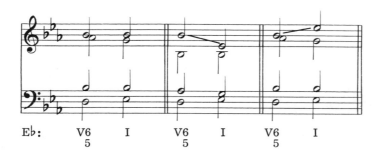

SECOND INVERSION

In the V_3^4 chord the second degree of the scale is found in the bass voice, again providing a smooth bass line. It supplies another harmonization to the second scale step when the bass moves from the third to the first degree. Previously the V_4^6 served in this capacity. In this case the V_3^4 will normally occur in an unaccented part of the measure and will serve the function of a passing chord. In the normal resolution, the voices move as in the V_7 chord—again, except for the root, which remains stationary. The normal resolution is to I. It may also move to another form of the V_7 chord.

Example 8–23.

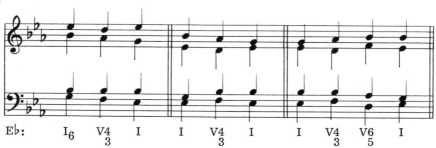

Example 8-24. SCHUBERT, Moment Musical, Op. 94, No. 2 (*Andante*).

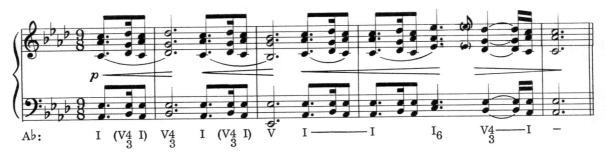

The V_3^4 chord may resolve to a I_6, if a less conclusive resolution is desired. In this progression, however, the seventh of the V_3^4 chord moves up one degree to the fifth of the following chord, thus providing a satisfactory doubling for the I_6.

Example 8-25.

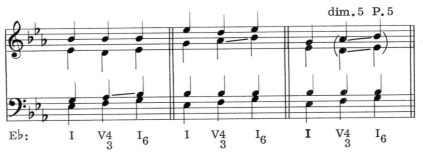

Example 8-26. BEETHOVEN, Sonata, Op. 31, No. 3 (*Allegretto vivace*).

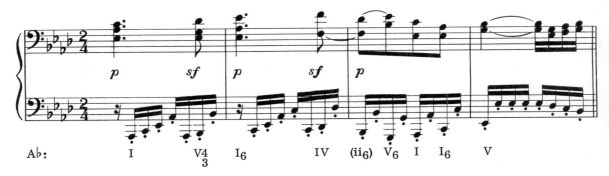

THIRD INVERSION

The V_2 chord is strong and more noticeably dissonant than the other inversions, because the characteristic tone in the chord—the seventh—is now found in the bass voice. For this reason the chord seventh must resolve down one degree to the third scale degree. The normal resolution of the V_2 will therefore be to I_6 rather than to I. It may also move to another form of the V_7 chord. Effective voice leading in this progression of V_2 to I_6 can be achieved by placing the fifth of the V_2 chord in the soprano voice and resolving it by moving it up an interval of a fourth to the fifth of the I_6.

Example 8–27.

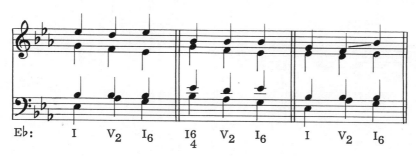

Example 8–28. BEETHOVEN, Sonata, Op. 13 (*Adagio cantabile*).

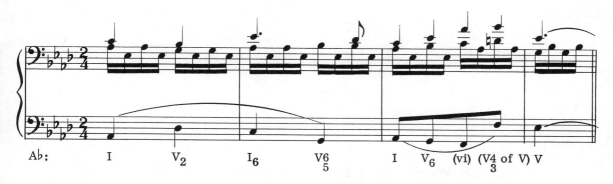

NOTE: Although not a resolution as such, one inversion may move to another inversion of the V_7 chord in root position before resolving to a form of I. This extends the effect of the dominant sound with added interest.

Example 8–29.   BEETHOVEN, Sonata, Op. 57 (*Andante con moto*).

Soprano Harmonization

Use the principles presented in earlier chapters for harmonizing a given soprano and add to the soprano chord selection table the following possibilities involving the V_7 chord and its inversions.

Example 8–30.

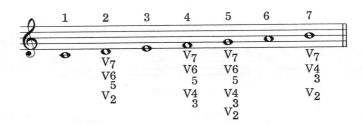

Keyboard Work Using the V_7 Chord and Its Inversions

In the progressions shown in Example 8–31, the V_7 chord and its inversions are written in a concentrated manner. In music one will seldom find them all in a single progression. The inversions of V_7 below are complete; observe that the bass tone is the only one missing from the chord in the treble. Study the difference in sound and effect of each of the inversions as they are played and note the interest and drive produced by these chords despite the apparent monotony in certain voices.

Example 8–31.

The Suspension

As the name implies, the suspension is a chord tone of one chord which continues to sound (is suspended) through the change of harmony, then resolves stepwise downward to a chord tone of the second chord. This is an effective device for developing smoothness and subtlety in a harmonic progression, yet producing a mild type of dissonance. The preparation of the suspension is usually on a rhythmically weak beat, with the suspension itself occurring on a strong beat and the resolution following on a weak beat.

Example 8–32.

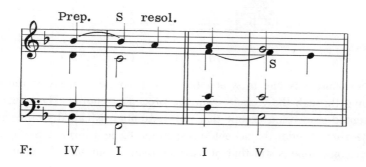

Example 8–33. SCHUMANN, Arabeske, Op. 18.

a: i   (ii°6)   i6   V7   i
                                     4

When this non-harmonic tone resolves upward, it is called a *retardation*.

Example 8–34.

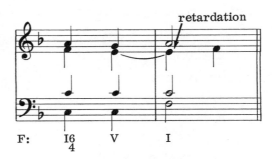

F: I6   V   I
          4

While we usually associate a suspension with a tie, the non-harmonic tone may occur within a measure with no tie but still with a weak-strong-weak rhythmic pattern being present.

Example 8–35.

F: I   IV   I

An *accented* suspension is one in which the tone is sounded again at the change of harmony rather than sounding through the change from the preceding chord. The effect of this is similar to that of the unaccented suspension except that more attention is called to the dissonance by accent. Although some theorists consider the accented suspension to be a form of the *appoggiatura,* the function of the non-harmonic tone is still that of carrying over a tone into the change of harmony.

Example 8–36. BEETHOVEN, Sonata, Op. 31, No. 3 (*Menuetto*).

The *indirect* suspension is an elaboration of the above types in which other tones are inserted between the suspension and its resolution. The indirect suspension provides many possibilities for variety and beauty in a melodic line. Observe the illustrations in Example 8–37 and experiment with different possibilities, since these are not limited as are the two types described above.

Example 8–37.

The open, hollow quality of parallel fifths can be subdued by creating a suspension in one of the two voices involved.

Example 8–38.

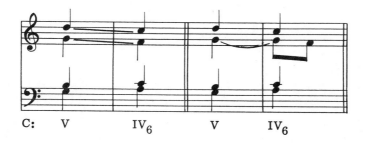

Assignments

1. Harmonize each of the following progressions in two ways in four-part chorale style. Use examples of both complete and incomplete V_7 chords:

   (a) I–IV–V_7–I in D major
   (b) i–V–V_7–i in f sharp minor
   (c) I–V_5^6–I–V_3^4–I–V_7–I in A flat major
   (d) i–i_6–V_2–i_6–V_3^4–i in g minor
   (e) I–V_3^4–I_6–IV–I_4^6–V_7–I in B major

2. As the instructor plays progressions involving the V_7 and its inversions, write the bass and soprano voices and identify and label the chords.

3. Identify and write the chord labels for progressions or musical excerpts involving V_7 and its inversions, as played by the instructor.

4. Play the progressions which appear in the keyboard work section in all major and minor keys. Non-pianists: Play these as illustrated, with a steady pulse. Pianists: Play these as illustrated, but add the non-harmonic tones studied thus far.

5. Play original progressions using chords presented up to now in keyboard style. Pianists may play these in a free style, perhaps that of a particular composer being studied.

6. Harmonize the following basses, using passing tones, neighboring tones, and suspensions. Label all chords and non-harmonic tones (use S for suspensions, AS for accented suspensions, and IS for indirect suspensions).

(a)

(b)

(c)

(d)

(e)

```
7       6   #   6       #   #   #4  6   #6      6           6   7
#               5                   2       4       5           4   #
```

(f) Unfigured bass.

7. Harmonize the following soprano melodies, using V_7 and its inversions and the other chords studied thus far. If desired, use non-harmonic tones other than those indicated in the lower voices or alter the soprano line to create others.

   (a)

   (b)

   (c)

   (d) Free style.

(e) Free style.

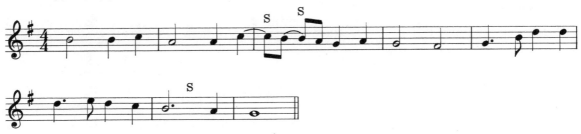

(f) ENGLISH, Drink to Me Only With Thine Eyes.

8. Play the following cadences in all major and minor keys in keyboard style. These are the cadences from assignment 7 of the previous chapter, with the V_7 replacing the V.

9. Sing the V_7 and its inversions in a suggested key or from a given note as illustrated:

10. Write one original exercise in major and one in minor, each including V_7 chords as well as the others studied, plus suspensions. Each must be at least eight measures in length.

11. Adapt and expand one of the completed exercises from assignment 6 or assignment 10 for voices, instruments, or piano in free style. Write for fewer or more than four parts.

12. Compose a free original composition in A B A form using V_7 chords and their inversions and suspensions. Each section should be eight measures in length. Include expression markings, dynamics indications, and tempo indications; perform it in class.

13. Analyze the following excerpts harmonically and stylistically, giving special attention to the V_7 and its inversions and the use of non-harmonic tones.

    (a) MOZART, Sonata (K283) (*Allegro*).

    (b) BACH, Freu' dich sehr, o meine Seele.

(c) BEETHOVEN, Sonata, Op. 110 (1st movement, measures 5–8).

(d) CHOPIN, Nocturne, Op. 37, No. 1 (*Andante sostenuto*).

(e) BEETHOVEN, Sonata, Op. 111 (2nd movement).

(f) SCHUBERT, Menuetto (*Allegro moderato*).

(g) BEETHOVEN, Sonata, Op. 10, No. 1 (*Allegro molto e con brio*).

(h) SCHUBERT, Impromptu, Op. 142, No. 2 (*Allegretto*).

14. In a similar manner, analyze, bring to class, and discuss music being studied which illustrates the material in this chapter.

9

SECONDARY TRIADS: SUPERTONIC, MEDIANT, SUBMEDIANT, LEADING TONE

Thus far in our study we have concentrated on the primary triads (tonic, subdominant, and dominant), because these three chords constitute the harmonic framework around which all tonal music is written. Inversions have been introduced, and the seventh chord built on the dominant tone has been studied, but this has been the extent to which variety has been achieved. It is obvious that music is not limited to these three basic sounds, but that others are introduced in the course of a composition for richness, color, and variety. These other triads are called *secondary* triads because, although they are important in a composition, they are of secondary importance to the structural harmony, the primary triads.

The secondary triads are the supertonic, the mediant, the submediant, and the leading tone triads. Each has its own characteristics and function.

Example 9–1.

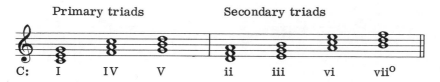

FUNCTION

The secondary triads constitute an elaboration of the primary triads within a composition. The skeletal movement in music is from I to V and back to I, so the relationship of the secondary triads is basically to I and V. There is also a relationship between the secondary triads and IV, but this, while basic, is of lesser importance in a harmonic progression. The secondary triads prolong or extend a given primary harmony or anticipate the primary harmony.

Because the primary triads in major keys are major triads, the secondary triads are useful in that they are minor or diminished, hence providing color and harmonic contrast to the work. In a similar sense, in minor keys the i and iv are minor and the V is major, while the secondary triads are as follows: ii° and vii° are diminished, and III and VI are major. Again the major-minor-diminished element of contrast is present.

Example 9–2.

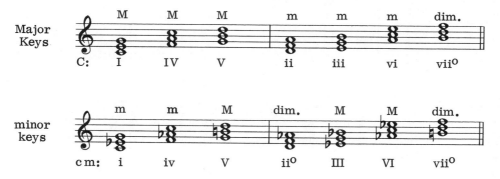

RELATIONSHIPS WITH PRIMARY TRIADS

Each secondary triad is functionally related to a specific primary triad, this relationship being similar to that of a minor key and its relative major key. The related primary triad is found a third above the secondary triad, so vi is related to I, iii is related to V, and ii is related to IV. The vii° chord has such strong dominant characteristics that it is related to the V rather than to ii. The significance of these relationships is that the secondary triad (vi, for example) is often used in addition to or as a substitute for its related primary triad (I in this example). The sound of the vi tends to extend or to color the I sound intended.

Example 9–3.

DOUBLING—TONAL AND MODAL DEGREES

In order to clarify the doubling procedure in all chords, including the secondary triads, it is essential to understand that certain scale degrees are more suitable for doubling than others, regardless of their position within the chord. As always, the determining factor is the sound, but the information below should facilitate the matter of doubling.

The tonic, dominant, subdominant, and supertonic scale degrees are called *tonal*, because they represent the foundation of a particular tonality and remain constant in major and minor keys. While the supertonic triad is not one of the primary triads, its role is an important one functionally because the second scale step lies in the relationship of the dominant of the dominant.

The mediant, submediant, and leading tone are called *modal* degrees because they determine the mode, at least partially, and do not basically affect the tonality. Triads built on these scale steps are variable and are often different in major and minor keys.

Example 9–4.

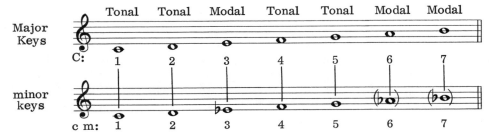

To achieve the most satisfactory balance of sound in a chord, it is advisable to double the root *or* a tonal degree in any of these chords. In the secondary triads, this will mean that the root or third of the chord is the preferred doubling, the choice being determined by the particular progression involved.

Example 9–5.

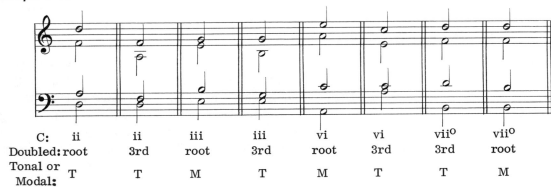

In primary triads this will mean that the root of the chord is the preferred tone to double, because it is both the root and a tonal degree. Next in preference will be the fifth, as it is also a tonal degree.

Example 9–6.

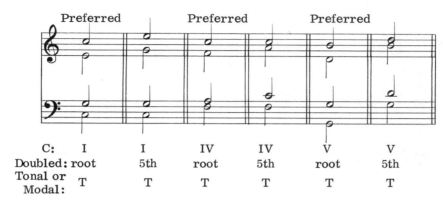

	C:	I	I	IV	IV	V	V
Doubled:	root		5th	root	5th	root	5th
Tonal or Modal:	T		T	T	T	T	T

We sometimes find tones other than the root or a tonal degree doubled. When this irregularity occurs, a specific type of voice leading or quality of sound has been the determining factor.

ROOT PROGRESSION

Progressions involving all chords are limited to three types: (a) those whose roots move a fifth up or down, (b) those whose roots move a third up or down, and (c) those whose roots move the interval of a second up or down. By its nature and characteristics, each type is distinctive and produces a progression noticeably different from another type.

A Fifth Up or Down. This is the strongest and most basic type of progression, the one which is the foundation of all tonal music (I–V–I). The two chords representing this type are related by having one tone in common which provides stability, and achieve contrast by the strong root movement of a fifth. Of the two progressions possible, up a fifth or down a fifth, the one creating more contrast is the *descending* fifth, as the root of the second chord is not found in the first chord. V–I can be considered a model of this type, with ii–V, I–IV, iii–vi and vi–ii also being effective.

Example 9–7.

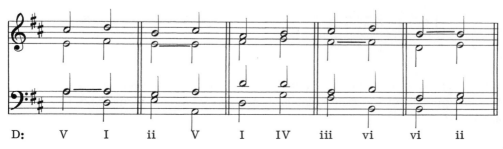

D: V   I   ii   V   I   IV   iii   vi   vi   ii

The progression *up* a fifth does not produce as much contrast as the descending fifth, but is still strong and effective. IV–I can serve as a model for this type, with ii–vi, I–V, and vi–iii also being effective. The other possibilities for each of these will be discussed under the specific chord.

Example 9–8.

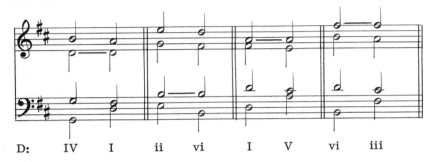

A Third Up or Down. The effect, musically, of this progression is not as strong as that of the movement of a fifth, because with two common tones and the smaller root interval of a third the contrast is less. However, there is often more color and smoothness in movement by a third, which is sometimes more desirable. Of the two progressions possible in this type, the strongest is that of the *descending* third, especially if the first of the two chords is one of the primary triads. In this instance the primary triad moves to its related secondary triad, extending the primary sound. I and vi can serve as a model for this type; IV–ii and V–iii are also satisfactory.

Example 9–9.

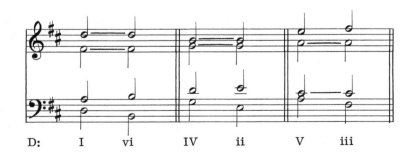

The effect of the progression *up* a third is weaker than the descending third. The only really satisfactory progressions of this type are I–iii, which can serve as a model, and, to a lesser degree, IV–vi and V–vii°.

Example 9–10.

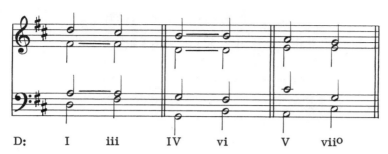

D: I   iii   IV   vi   V   vii°

A Second Up or Down. The effect of this progression is different from either of the other two because, while it produces more contrast than the others due to the lack of a common tone between the chords, the root movement is that of only one scale step. This type is more limited than the others. Of the two progressions possible in this type, the one moving *up* a second is generally more effective because more tension and direction are produced. IV–V can serve as a model, with V–vi (which will be useful in a cadential manner) and iii–IV also being satisfactory. I–ii, ii–iii, and vi–vii° are less satisfactory.

Example 9–11.

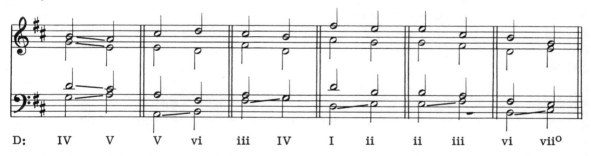

D: IV   V   V   vi   iii   IV   I   ii   ii   iii   vi   vii°

The effect of the progression *down* a second is weak and should be avoided, except possibly vi–V, V–IV, and I–vii° (as the tonic may progress to any chord).

Example 9–12.

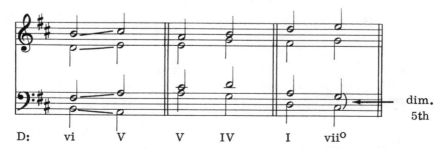

D: vi   V   V   IV   I   vii°

dim.
5th

NOTE: The use of inversions of these chords provides more flexibility and variety in the selection of harmonic possibilities.

Specific Secondary Triads

In the following discussion the particular characteristics and functions of each of the secondary triads are presented, first in terms of root position chords and then in the chords in the first inversion. Doubling in the first inversion of these triads is the same as in the corresponding triads in root position.

SUPERTONIC (ii IN MAJOR, ii° IN MINOR)

This triad is related to the IV chord, as was discussed above (see page 111). It is the most frequently used of the secondary triads and is the only one which has as its root a tonal degree of the scale. The ii may either follow the IV or appear as a substitute for it, but it may not precede the IV with effectiveness because a retrograde motion would result and the tonal strength of the progression would be lessened.

The principal function of the ii chord is that of a preparation for the V, this being especially good when the ii is used in place of the IV or between the IV and V in an authentic cadence. Sometimes it leads into the V by means of I_6. While the common tone may be kept in the same voice in this progression, this principle is often disregarded, with the upper three voices descending and the bass usually ascending. While used in both major and minor, the ii° is less often found in minor in root position, where it is a diminished triad.

Example 9–13.

Example 9–14. BACH, Heut' triumphieret Gottes Sohn.

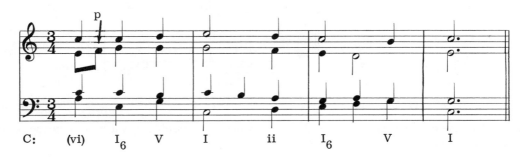

Example 9–15. Mozart, Sonata in B flat (K333) (*Allegro*).

Bb: I   (vi₆)   ii   V₇   I

MEDIANT (iii IN MAJOR, III IN MINOR)

This triad is related to the V and is used occasionally as a substitute for the V or it may follow it. The iii is not as useful a chord as the ii, but its main function is to lead to other chords which serve as connecting links between the iii and V. In a sense it is a transition chord, being dependent on stronger chords on either side. It may be inserted between I and IV or between vi and IV and is most effective in these progressions when the soprano line moves from 8 to 7 to 6 in the scale. It may also appear between V and vi to delay slightly the effect of the V.

Example 9–16.   Bourgeois, Old Hundredth.

Ab: I   iii   IV   I   G: I   (vi)   iii   IV   I   (vi)   V   I

In minor keys the mediant triad usually appears as a major triad (III), employing the natural minor mode for the fifth of the chord. This chord is effective because it suggests the tonic chord of the relative major key, yet maintains the role of the mediant. When the mediant appears as III⁺, an augmented triad caused by the raised seventh scale step, it is striking in sound but much more limited in its use and usually resolves up a fourth to the VI chord.

Example 9–17.

SUBMEDIANT (vi IN MAJOR, VI IN MINOR)

This triad is related to the I, and for that reason is nearly as free in its possibilities as the tonic. The vi is used normally as a substitute for the I or to follow I, but not to progress to I, as this would be a retrogression. In major this chord is a minor triad (vi) and in minor it is major (VI), so it can be used successfully in either mode to counteract the prevailing effect. In addition to the illustration below, those for ii contain examples of vi also.

Example 9–18.

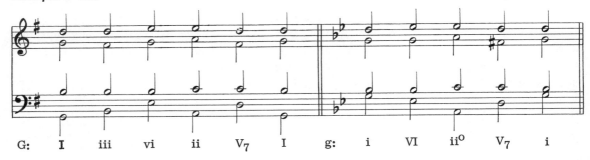

Deceptive Cadence. A cadence, usually authentic, in which the final tonic chord is replaced by another chord is called a deceptive cadence. There are several possibilities for this final chord, but by far the most frequent final chord is the vi. When the V–vi progression is heard instead of V–I in a cadential progression, the phrase ending is felt but the sound is not conclusive. In this progression the root and third move up and the other two voices move down, resulting in a vi with a doubled third.

Example 9–19.

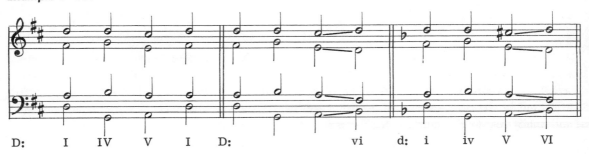

Example 9–20. Mozart, Fantasia in d minor (*Allegretto*).

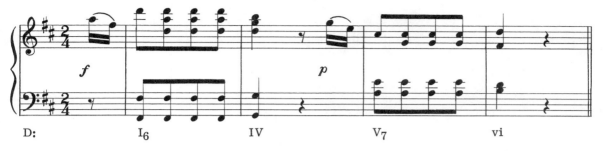

LEADING TONE (vii° IN MAJOR AND MINOR, SOMETIMES VII IN MINOR)

The leading tone triad is seldom used in root position except in a sequential passage, because it is a diminished triad in both major and minor modes, thereby lacking strength and independence. When it is used as a substitute for the V, a tone other than the root (leading tone) is doubled and its normal resolution is to the tonic chord. When it progresses by root movement of a fifth to iii in major keys, the leading tone is doubled, because now the root is not serving in the capacity of a "leading" tone. When it progresses in minor keys to III, the leading tone triad appears as VII, a major triad formed by the lowering of the seventh degree as found in the natural minor scale. This produces a strong feeling of the relative major key, as was suggested in the discussion on III.

Example 9–21.

SECONDARY SIX-CHORDS

The function and usefulness of secondary triads in the first inversion is often different from that of the same triads in root position. The fact that the third of the chord is in the bass seems to make more difference in secondary triads than in some of the other chords.

The ii₆ is often a more successful chord in a harmonic progression than the ii in root progression, because it has a stronger sense of motion and a lighter texture. It may be used in most places where a ii is possible, and often follows the tonic, which the ii normally does not. Its main function is to help form a cadential pattern.

Example 9-22.

Eb:　　I　(vi)　IV　V　I　　　　ii6　　　　I　ii6　V　I

Example 9-23. BEETHOVEN, Sonata, Op. 28 (*Scherzo*).

D:　　　　　　I　　ii6　　V7　　I

The iii6 is harmonically weak and suggests V with a non-harmonic tone a sixth above the root. It demands resolution to the V by the movement of just one note. This chord is not often used, but when it is used, stronger harmonies should support it.

Example 9-24.

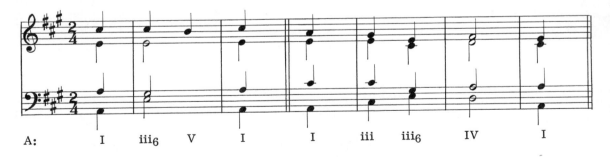

A:　　I　iii6　V　I　　I　iii　iii6　IV　I

The vi6 is similar to the iii6 in suggesting the use of non-harmonic tones, this one being a tonic with a sixth above the root instead of the fifth. The vi6 is seldom used as an independent chord because of this weakness, but when it is used it usually resolves to ii. In this progression the root movement is that of a fifth.

Example 9–25.

The vii°$_6$ is a very valuable chord which is widely used as a substitute for V. It has dominant characteristics plus a more workable form with the third (second scale step) in the bass. It is also effectively used as a passing chord between I and I$_6$.

Example 9–26.

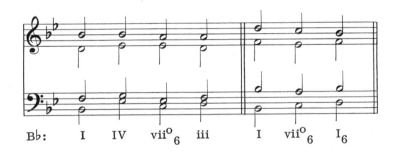

Example 9–27. SCHUMANN, Soldier's March.

CONSECUTIVE SIX-CHORDS

If consecutive six-chords are used, including both primary and secondary triads, it is advisable to change the doubling in alternate chords to insure contrary motion and melodic interest in each part and also to avoid parallel fifths and octaves.

Example 9–28.

SOPRANO HARMONIZATION OF SECONDARY TRIADS

The same principles as applied earlier will be used to harmonize a given soprano part in which secondary triads and their first inversions are used.

Example 9–29.

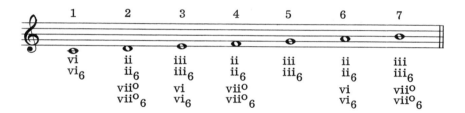

SECONDARY SIX-FOUR CHORDS

The second inversion of secondary triads is seldom found in music of the common practice period. If it is used, and this will usually be in a sequential pattern, its normal resolution is to a triad whose root is the same as the bass note of the six-four chord preceding it. The effect here will be that of non-harmonic tones over a stationary bass.

KEYBOARD WORK USING SECONDARY TRIADS

Employ the same procedure for keyboard work as was presented in the previous chapters. Now, however, add the secondary triads in root position and in the first inversion. Augment the basic style with a more pianistic one in the following ways.

1. Play the bass note of the chord with the left hand on the main accent, then follow with a chord completing the harmony of that chord, while the right hand plays the melody. In $\frac{3}{4}$ time there will be one bass note followed by two chords, etc. Include the melody note in the chord structure for principles of doubling and balance.

Example 9–30.

2. Use a figure such as the one in Example 9–31 to create a smoother bass part. This device is frequently used in piano music.

Example 9–31.

3. Use one or the other of the above types and add non-harmonic tones to the accompaniment.

Example 9–32.

The Anticipation

The anticipation is an unaccented non-harmonic tone which belongs to the second of two chords but is sounded before the second chord is heard. As the name implies, it anticipates the chord to which it belongs. Thus the anticipation is the opposite of the suspension. Example 9–33 illustrates a basic two-chord progression (1), a suspension inserted in this progression (2), and an anticipation inserted in the same basic progression (3). Although an anticipation is usually approached by a step, it may be approached by a skip (4).

Example 9–33.

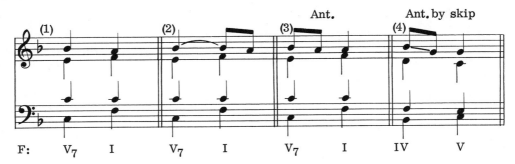

The example shows a *direct* anticipation, the most frequently used type, in which the note of resolution is the same as the anticipation itself. The *indirect* anticipation does not remain on the same note but resolves to another chord tone by a skip.

Example 9–34.

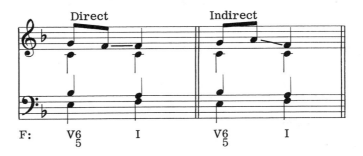

When the anticipation is used, the normal principles of voice leading and doubling are maintained as though there were no non-harmonic tone present.

Assignments

NOTE: The assignments preceded by an asterisk (*) are intended for the student who has studied the first part of this chapter (up to "Secondary Six-Chords") after having studied Chapter 5. Students who have studied all the preceding chapters consecutively should be expected to do all or any of the exercises.

1. Harmonize each of the following progressions in two ways in four-part chorale style:

    *(a) I–iii–IV–ii–V–I in A major
    *(b) i–VI–ii°–V–VI in f minor
    *(c) I–IV–ii–V–iii–IV–V–I in D flat major

(d) i–i$_6$–iv–ii$^\circ_6$–i$^6_4$–V$_7$–i in b minor

(e) I–IV–vii$^\circ$–iii–IV–V$^4_3$–I in E flat major

(f) I–vi–IV–ii–I$^6_4$–V$_7$–I in G flat major

*2. Listen to secondary triads as they are played in a progression and learn to recognize the distinguishing characteristics of each. As progressions including secondary triads are played, write the bass and soprano voices, then label the chords. Secondary triads should be learned first in root position; when these have been mastered, the first inversion should be added.

*3. Identify and write chord labels for progressions or musical excerpts involving these secondary triads, as played by the instructor.

4. Play the progressions which appear in the keyboard work section in all keys of the mode of the Examples. Non-pianists: Play these as written with a steady pulse. Pianists: Add non-harmonic tones, including the anticipation.

5. Non-pianists: Play original progressions in piano style using the chords presented thus far and experimenting with simple accompaniment patterns. Pianists: Play original progressions in the style of the accompaniment patterns suggested, first working out the progression, then adding a melodic line and an accompaniment figure.

6. Harmonize the following basses in chorale style, using non-harmonic tones studied thus far. Label all chords and non-harmonic tones (the label for the anticipation is "Ant." and for the indirect anticipation, "I Ant.").

*(a)

*(b)

*(c)

(d)

(e)

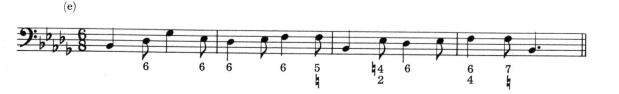

(f)

(g)

(h) Unfigured bass.

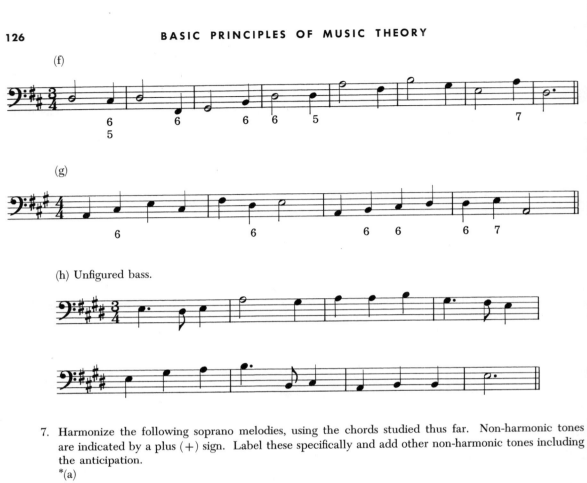

7. Harmonize the following soprano melodies, using the chords studied thus far. Non-harmonic tones are indicated by a plus (+) sign. Label these specifically and add other non-harmonic tones including the anticipation.

*(a)

*(b)

*(c)

(d)

(e)

(f)

(g)

(h)

(i)

(j) BACH, Freu'dich sehr, o meine Seele.

8. Sing each of the secondary triads in a given key, using the tonic tone as the point of departure:
   *(a)

G: ii   iii   vi   vii⁰

Sing each of the secondary triads in a given key in root position and in the first inversion, beginning on the root, then the third:

(b)

9. Write one original exercise in major and one in minor, each including secondary triads in root position and in the first inversion. Each must be at least eight measures in length. Use anticipations.

10. Compose a free composition in any medium in which you experiment with the material presented in this chapter. (The length of this work is to be determined by the instructor.)

11. Analyze the following excerpts harmonically and stylistically, giving special attention to the use of secondary triads:

(a) SCHUBERT, Sonata, Op. 143 (*Andante*) (ending).

(b) KUHNAU, Biblical Sonata No. 1 (6th movement).

Allegretto tranquillo

(c) MARPURG, Menuet.

Allegretto grazioso

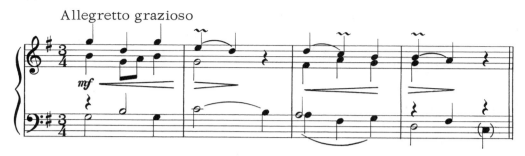

(d) GALUPPI, Sonata in D (1st movement).

Adagio

(e) BEETHOVEN, Sonatina in G (*Romanza*) (two excerpts).

(f) HANDEL, Allegro in G.

12. In a similar manner, analyze, bring to class, and discuss music being studied which illustrates the material in this chapter.

10
MODULATION

The idea of key sense or tonality has been stressed from the beginning of this course of study, because it is the element that ties music together and produces unity. A work that consists of more than a few measures will have unity but will lack interest and become dull if it is based solely on the harmonic vocabulary in one key. A change of key within a composition will produce interest, contrast, and harmonic color, will intensify the feeling of motion, and will make an effective extended work possible. This technique of changing the key center is known as *modulation,* and is found in all compositions of any extended length.

ELEMENTS OF MODULATION

An effective modulation involves much more than simply changing the tonal center. The elements of rhythm, melody, and form contribute in an important manner to the true essence of modulation, and it must be kept in mind that, to make it meaningful, a musical reason and need must exist for changing the key center.

OCCURRENCE

A modulation is most often found at the end of a phrase or section of a composition, although sometimes it is found at the beginning of a section. In the sonata form of the classical period the first main section, called the "exposition," usually ends in the key of the dominant if in major and in the relative major key if in minor. Considering a musical work as a whole, the usual procedure is to return to the original key at the end of the work after having modulated to at least one different key during the course of the work.

TYPES

There are several different methods of changing keys, the choice being determined by the over-all style of the composition, by the amount of attention to be drawn to the key change, and by the harmonic vocabulary being used. The more complex types of modulatory procedure are those involving modal alteration, enharmonic equivalents, sequence, common tone, chromaticism, and a variety called "abrupt." These will be discussed in Chapter 16. The most frequently used and the most direct is called the "pivot chord" type of modulation.

Pivot Chord Modulation

DESCRIPTION

In any modulation three principal ideas are essential. These are purely harmonic, and are in addition to the "Elements of Modulation" discussed at the beginning of this chapter. First is the establishment of the original key, then the point of transition, and finally the establishment of the new key. It is at the point of transition that the differences in types of modulation occur, and in this type of key change the pivot represents the transition.

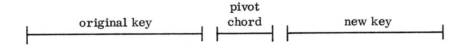

ORIGINAL KEY

It is important that the original key be well established so that the ear senses a feeling of a real tonal center. This key sense is accomplished most securely by the presence of an authentic cadence. The length of the section in the original key will vary from several measures to many, according to the composition.

TRANSITION

In the pivot chord type of modulation, the transition consists of a chord which can be interpreted as belonging to both the original key and the key of destination. On pages 29–30 the key relationship of triads is discussed. By reviewing this material, one will discover that a specific major triad may belong to eight different keys. Theoretically, this specific major triad may serve as a pivot chord to seven other keys, but it will be discovered in the examples below that some key relationships will prove to be more musically satisfying than others.

Example 10–1.

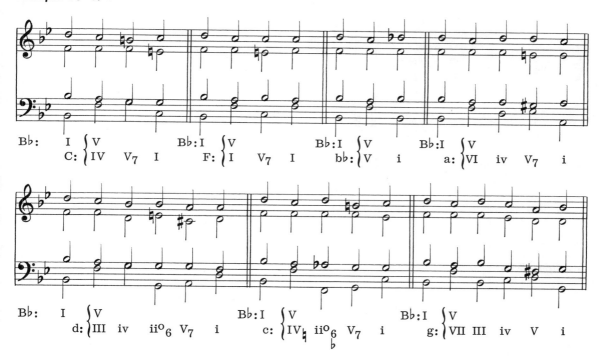

In the modulation from B flat major to b flat minor, what actually takes place is a change of mode (the parallel minor) rather than a change of key. In the modulation from B flat major to g minor the pivot chord is actually the III or iv of the new key of g minor rather than the chord indicated. This modulation has been written as shown in Example 10–1 because of the normal harmonic progression from VII in the key of g minor.

A *minor* triad in any key may theoretically be a pivot chord in modulating to five other keys. (See Example 10–2.)

A *diminished* triad may be an effective pivot chord in modulating to the relative key only. Here the first inversion of the diminished triad is preferred, as was discussed in Chapter 9, instead of the triad in root position. (See Example 10–3.)

Example 10–2.

Example 10–3.

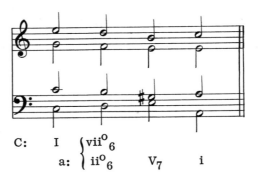

The pivot chord may be any chord in the original key which will serve this purpose, but preferably not the V of the key of destination. Also, inversions are as useful as chords in root position for use as pivot chords.

Instead of one pivot chord, several pivot chords in succession may be possible, each being interpreted as belonging to the original key and the key of destination. When this occurs, the last of the pivot chords is usually considered the actual pivot chord unless previous chords help to form the authentic cadence in the new key. No feeling of key change is felt during the pivot chord transition, but only when a chord foreign to the original key is heard.

Example 10–4.

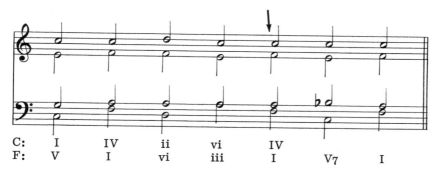

NEW KEY

After the pivot chord transition the establishment of the new key is accomplished by means of a cadence in that new key. The most effective cadences for this use are the authentic and half cadences. The section of the composition in the new key must be long enough to establish the new tonality firmly. The V or, better yet, the V_7 in this cadence is the chord producing the most intensity to give this feeling of a key change.

Example 10–5.

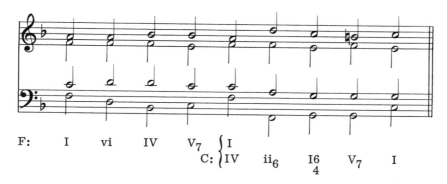

SELECTION OF A NEW KEY

The most frequently used modulation is to the dominant key if the original key is major, or to the *relative major* key if the original key is minor. Modulation to any of the closely related keys is also effective. A closely related key has one more (or less) flat or sharp in the key signature than the original key and also includes the relative keys of those with one more (or less) flat or sharp. Example 10–6 illustrates the keys closely related to C major.

Example 10–6.

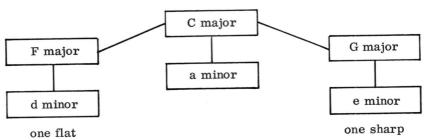

one flat   one sharp

Modulation to a remote key, in which no diatonic pivot chord is available between the two keys, is possible by the use of an intermediate key. To accomplish this, the first modulation is to a more closely related key possessing a pivot chord, and the second modulation is from this intermediate key to the remote key by the same means.

Example 10–7.

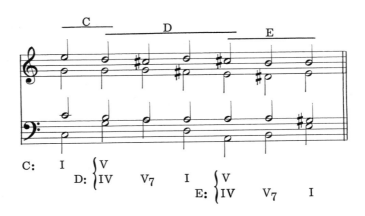

Keyboard Work Involving Modulation

In playing a phrase which modulates to a closely related key, first select a pivot chord and remember its function in both keys. Now, establish the original key as presented in the discussion earlier in this chapter and *think* the pivot chord as it is played in the original key. While playing the pivot chord, shift your thinking so that this same chord now belongs and has meaning to you in the new key. Complete the phrase with an authentic cadence, thinking in the new key. Develop unity within the phrase by rhythmic coherence and a melodic contour which makes musical sense.

In the brief examples below the first two measures establish the key of C, the tonic chord at the end of the second measure being the pivot chord. In the first illustration, the pivot chord is IV in the key of G; in the second, the pivot chord is V in the key of F, and in the third, the pivot chord is VI in the key of e minor. From the pivot chord to the end of each phrase the new key is established by an authentic cadence. These examples should serve as a starting point for modulations to other keys using the same pivot chord and also for modulations using other pivot chord possibilities.

Example 10–8.

Harmonic Rhythm

In Chapter 4 meter and rhythm were discussed in terms of melodic writing. As musical works are studied, one is made aware of the nature of harmonic backgrounds in ways which are beyond basic meter and chord structure. *Harmonic rhythm* consists of the underlying rhythmic aspects of music and is concerned with two main principles: (a) the frequency of harmonic change, and (b) the rhythmic quality of that change in terms of accents. This, in turn, is related to the quality of sound produced by harmonic progressions. It is one of the vital aspects of music, and its study is appropriate at this time because of the rhythmic and musical elements of modulation.

FREQUENCY OF HARMONIC CHANGE

On page 57 we learned that in some music one harmony will be maintained through one or more consecutive measures, while in other music, such as the chorale, the harmony frequently changes on each beat. These represent the two extremes. Most music falls somewhere between these two in regard to the frequency of harmonic change.

Analyze the Beethoven excerpt in Example 10–9 on this basis. The first six measures are basically one chord per measure, with the vii$_6$ occurring in measures 1 and 3 as passing chords. Measures 7 and 8 contain two chords which form the half cadence.

Example 10–9. BEETHOVEN, Sonata, Op. 49, No. 1.

The harmonic plan of this excerpt is shown in Example 10–10.

Example 10–10.

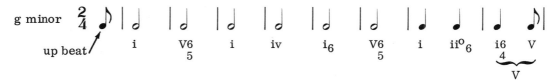

RHYTHMIC QUALITY OF HARMONIC CHANGE

The Beethoven example above illustrates a regular rhythmic pattern as regards harmonic change. The principal accent of each measure introduces a sound not heard in the preceding measure so that each chord extends in time from one main accent to another. In measure 7 the ii$_6^{\circ}$ appears on the second beat to prepare for the approaching cadence, and in measure 8 the i$_4^6$ serves its cadential function as a dependent chord resolving to the V. The waltz is an excellent example of this regular pattern of harmonic change, for here the intended accent on the first beat of the measure is usually intensified by a change of harmony.

The bass quarter note on the first beat of each measure in the Chopin excerpt in Example 10–11 indicates and establishes the position of the harmony for the entire measure, in spite of the fact that its duration is only one beat. The chords on the second and third beats complete the harmony of each measure. For example, in measure 1 the second and third beats would not be considered I$_4^6$ chords, but the tonic chord in root position would be felt throughout the measure.

Example 10–11. CHOPIN, Valse in A flat, Op. 34, No. 1.

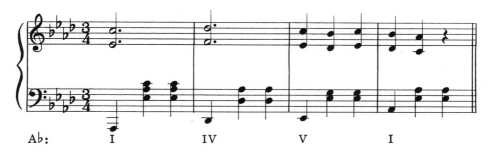

The Brahms excerpt (Example 10–12) illustrates an irregular rhythmic pattern of harmonic change. While the second measure is regular, the first measure contains a secondary accent on the second and fifth beats rather than on the third and sixth. The duple rhythmic nature of the measure is still maintained, however. The quality of the V and iii in the first measure is that of a pulling and an urgency toward the vi and iv, respectively.

Example 10–12. BRAHMS, Romanza, Op. 118, No. 5.

MELODIC RHYTHM

This consists of the rhythmic structure of a melody and may or may not coincide with the harmonic rhythm discussed above. In the Brahms (Example 10–12), the melodic rhythm and the harmonic rhythm coincide, except for the third beat of the second measure where the melodic tone is repeated. The outline of this would be as follows:

Example 10–13.

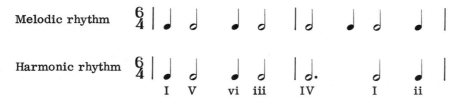

The Beethoven example (see Example 10-9), however, illustrates the type in which the melodic rhythm does not coincide with the harmonic rhythm.

Example 10-14.

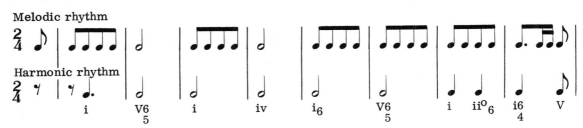

Melodic rhythm

Harmonic rhythm

One of these types is not necessarily preferred over the other, but the choice is determined by period, style, tempo, harmonic selection, meter, and, in the final analysis, the idea in the mind of the composer. The composer does not usually think of this element consciously; his creative instinct dictates the type of melodic and harmonic rhythm he will use.

The value of this study of harmonic rhythm lies in the fact that music is made up of elements which go beyond basic harmonic progressions. Through the study of harmonic rhythm it is possible to derive more insight into the musical language of the individual composer.

The *Appoggiatura*

The *appoggiatura* is an *accented* non-harmonic tone which is approached by a skip and resolved stepwise, usually in the opposite direction. The word itself is derived from the Italian *"appoggiare,"* meaning "to lean," and the effect in sound is one of a tone foreign to a harmony leaning or moving with pressure into the chord of resolution.

Example 10-15.

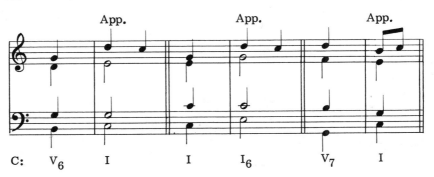

Example 10–16. WAGNER, March, from "Tannhauser."

C: I   I₆   vi —   ii₆   I⁶₄   V₇   I

The most striking characteristic of this non-harmonic tone is that of the unprepared dissonance, often chromatic. This feature made it especially adaptable to music of the classical and romantic periods. Some theorists refer to any accented non-harmonic tone as an *appoggiatura*, such as the accented passing tone or the suspension which is not tied or held over. We will use the more specific interpretation, however, because of the nature of the dissonance. It is one of the most effective non-harmonic tones because it is dramatic and stimulates movement, and its suddenness creates excitement and color.

Assignments

1. Harmonize the following phrases, modulating where indicated:

    (a) Key of C: I–IV–ii₆–V₇–⎰I
                G: ⎱IV–ii–I⁶₄–V₇–I
    (b) Key of E flat: I–vi–IV–ii–⎰V
                   F:⎱ IV–I–ii₆–V₇–I
    (c) Key of g minor: i–III–iv–V₇–i–⎰iv
                B flat: ⎱ii–I⁶₄–V₇–I

2. Listen to modulating progressions as they are played and determine the new key and the means of modulation. Using the procedure previously employed, write the bass, then the soprano, and finally the chord labels.

3. Play the progressions which appear in the keyboard work section in all keys, thinking the pivot chord first in the original key and then in the new key before progressing.

4. Using the first two measures of the above keyboard progression (see Example 10–8), devise pivot chord modulations to keys other than those presented.

5. Non-pianists: Play original modulating progressions, following the procedures set forth in this chapter. Pianists: Play original modulating progressions in free piano style of your own choosing. All students should include examples of the *appoggiatura*.

6. Harmonize the following figured basses in chorale style, using the *appoggiatura* where appropriate (label "App." for *appoggiatura*).

    (a)

(b)

(c)

7. Harmonize the following modulating soprano melodies, using the chords studied thus far. Non-harmonic tones are indicated by a plus sign. Label these specifically and add non-harmonic tones in the other voices where they will contribute musically to the exercise.

(a)

(b)

(c)

(d) BACH, *Ach Gott, wie manches Herzeleid.*

(e) BACH, Heut'triumphieret Gottes Sohn.

(f) From BEETHOVEN, Tune (Germany).

8. Write one original modulating exercise in major and one in minor, each utilizing the harmonic resources now at your disposal. Each must be at least eight measures in length.

9. Analyze the following excerpts harmonically and stylistically, noting particularly the means of modulation.

(a) BACH, Gavotte, from Fifth French Suite.

(b) BEETHOVEN, Sonata, Op. 2, No. 1 (*Menuetto*).

(c) MOZART, Sonata (K282) (*Menuetto I*).

(d) MOZART, Fantasie in d minor (*Allegretto*).

(e) SCHUMANN, Sicilienne.

(f) BEETHOVEN, Sonata, Op. 10, No. 3 (*Presto*).

10. Reduce one or more of the excerpts in assignment 9 to the harmonic rhythm and melodic rhythm patterns. Now write an original work based on the harmonic formula and harmonic rhythm of the excerpt but using an original style and melodic rhythm. Experiment also with retaining the original melodic rhythm.

11. Compose a free composition in any medium, experimenting with the material presented in this chapter. (The length of the work is to be determined by the instructor.)

12. Analyze, bring to class, and discuss modulating excerpts found in music being studied. Be sure these excerpts contain the pivot chord type of modulation. Bring to class for discussion examples of the *appoggiatura*.

11

THE SECONDARY DOMINANT

Most of the accidentals found in the music of the common practice period are caused by the presence of a dominant or dominant seventh chord of another key which is added to the harmonic texture of the original key for chromatic interest. Modulation, as was presented in Chapter 10, constitutes a definite change of tonal center, while these chords, called "secondary dominants," consist of a momentary departure from a given key. With this sound we enter the realm of chromaticism.

Any diatonic major or minor triad, other than the tonic, may be considered a temporary tonic and may be preceded by its own dominant triad or dominant seventh chord. This secondary dominant, while standing in the relationship of the dominant to the tonic, is a chord foreign to the key itself.

While we will refer to these chords as secondary dominants, some theorists prefer to call them apparent seventh chords, altered chords, transient modulations, borrowed chords, or applied dominant relationships. The information below should validate the term "secondary dominant."

TERMINOLOGY

Chord labels for these chords will correspond to their dominant function. For example, if the V is to be preceded by its own V_7, the figured bass symbol would be V_7 of V. It could also be considered a ii_7 with a raised third, but here the dominant relationship would not be clear. We will use the former symbol (V_7 of V), although the chord will sound the same with either nomenclature.

Example 11–1.

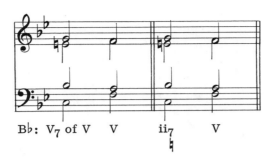

Bb: V₇ of V   V   ii₇   V

Example 11–2 illustrates the possible secondary dominant seventh chords in root position in the key of C major. Each triad in this key is preceded by its own dominant seventh chord. Note that vii° is not included in the example because, as a diminished triad, it could not become a temporary tonic. The upper level of chord symbols indicates the nomenclature in terms of the key of C, while the lower level indicates the same progression in the temporary key.

Example 11–2.

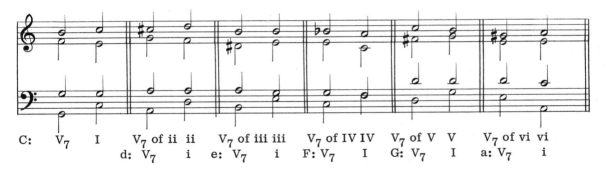

C: V₇ I   V₇ of ii ii   V₇ of iii iii   V₇ of IV IV   V₇ of V V   V₇ of vi vi
        d: V₇   i   e: V₇   i   F: V₇   I   G: V₇   I   a: V₇   i

HISTORICAL DEVELOPMENT

Secondary dominant chords have been used since the pre-Bach era. Bach and his contemporaries made extensive use of them to enhance and intensify harmonically the diatonic melodic line in the music of their period. Even such works as the Chorales of Bach contain numerous examples of these chords. They were used freely from this period through the nineteenth century. In the music of our own time, while not being an important element in the contemporary style, the secondary dominants have found a valuable place in popular music.

In the baroque and classical periods these chords were frequently used at the end of a phrase in a composition in the form of the V of V to strengthen the dominant in a half cadence and also to suggest a modulation, which may or may not have followed. The following excerpt from a Bach chorale will illustrate this point.

Example 11–3. BACH, Das walt' mein Gott.

STRUCTURE

The secondary dominant may be the V, V_7, or the vii° (V_7 without the root) in structure, and may appear in root position or in an inversion. Any tone in the chord may appear in the soprano voice. Later we will discover that the vii°$_7$ and other forms of the dominant may also be used.

Example 11–4.

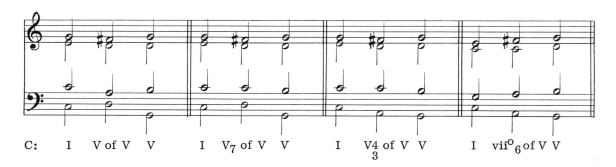

These secondary dominants may be recognized in the following ways:

1. At least one accidental will be present (the raised leading tone in minor being taken for granted), because these are triads or seventh chords foreign to the key. If there are no accidentals the chord in question can be interpreted in the original key.

2. The structure will be that of a major triad, a dominant seventh chord, or a diminished triad, as in the case of the vii°.

Example 11–5. BACH, In dich hab' ich gehoffet, Herr.

B♭:   I   V₇   vi   V₆   V₇   V⁶₅ of vi   vi   V⁶₅ of V   V₇   I

FUNCTION

These chords are used to lend color to the harmonic texture and to strengthen the tonality, because the secondary dominant emphasizes its chord of resolution without resulting in a modulation. While they increase the feeling of movement, these chords are less forceful than the regular dominants, because the resolution is to a chord other than the tonic in the key. Thus the basic V to I progression is achieved while focusing attention on these other steps of the scale. This gives direction to a musical progression.

The most frequently used secondary dominants are the V of V and the V of ii. The V of IV in major is not possible, as this would be simply the tonic triad, but the V₇ of IV is possible as a secondary dominant, because the chord would include the lowered seventh degree of the scale.

PREPARATION

Any diatonic triad may precede the secondary dominant. A smooth harmonic effect will result if the chord is preceded by a triad which belongs to both the original key and that of the secondary dominant. Any normal progression will be enhanced by the use of one of these chords, and a progression which is considered ineffective can be strengthened and even justified by the insertion of a secondary dominant chord.

Example 11–6.

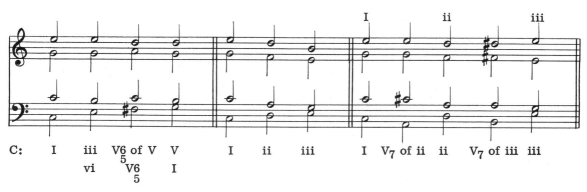

C: I   iii   V⁶₅ of V   V   I   ii   iii   I   V₇ of ii   ii   V₇ of iii   iii
             vi   V⁶₅   I

RESOLUTION

The secondary dominant chord normally resolves to its own tonic (major or minor), which in turn is a diatonic triad in the original key. For example, the V_7 of iii would resolve to its tonic which would be iii in the original key. Irregular resolutions are possible also, so if the equivalent of V_7–vi were desired, the progression of V_7 of vi would resolve to IV instead of vi. The voice leading and doubling of the secondary dominant is the same as for the regular V, V_7, or vii^{o}_6.

Example 11–7.

The chromatically altered tones are not doubled, and those which are chromatically raised resolve upward while those which are lowered resolve downward.

SPECIFIC SECONDARY DOMINANTS

The following discussion of these chords will serve to pinpoint the characteristics of each. The V_7 and vii_6 as secondary dominant chords are included under each basic heading.

V of II. Possible only in major keys, as in minor the supertonic triad is diminished, it normally resolves to ii. The root is the sixth step of the scale, and the altered tone is the raised tonic, which resolves up one step.

Example 11–8.

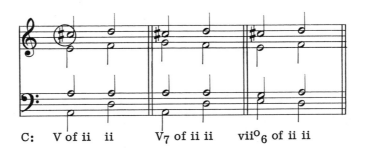

V of III. Possible in both major and minor keys, it normally resolves to iii (III), and its root is the leading tone. In major keys there are two altered tones, the raised supertonic and subdominant (the third and fifth of the chord). In minor keys there is no alteration, as the root is the lowered leading tone (the seventh step in the natural minor scale), thereby producing the effect of an altered tone in the harmonic minor scale.

Example 11–9.

C: V of iii iii   V₇ of iii iii   vii°₆ of iii iii   a: V of III III   V₇ of III III   vii°₆ of III III

V of IV. This chord is possible in both major and minor keys, but not possible as the V of IV in major, because this is the tonic triad and needs no further analysis. The normal resolution is to IV (iv). In major keys the altered tone is the lowered seventh of the scale which, in turn, is the seventh of the chord. This is the only lowered alteration in major key secondary dominant chords. In the vii°₆ of IV the lowered alteration resolves upward, contrary to the usual practice. In minor keys the third scale step is raised and the leading tone is lowered from the harmonic minor form (the third of the chord is raised and the seventh of the chord is lowered).

Example 11–10.

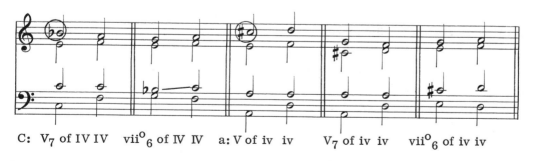

C: V₇ of IV IV   vii°₆ of IV IV   a: V of iv iv   V₇ of iv iv   vii°₆ of iv iv

V of V. This chord, the most frequently used of all secondary dominants, is not only possible in both major and minor keys, but is the only chord of this type which resolves to a major triad in either mode. Its normal resolution is to V. In major keys the fourth of the scale (the third of the chord) is raised, and in minor keys both the fourth and the sixth of the scale (third and fifth of the chord) are raised.

Example 11–11.

C: V of V V   V6/5 of V V   vii°6 of V V   a: V of V V   V4/3 of V V   vii°6 of V V

V of VI. Possible in both major and minor keys, this chord resolves normally to vi in major and VI in minor. Its root is the mediant step of the scale. In major keys the fifth scale step is raised (third of the chord), and in minor keys the leading tone (fifth of the chord) is left unaltered and the second scale step (seventh of the chord) is lowered. Contrary to the usual practice, the lowered second step resolves upward in the progression vii°6 of VI to VI.

Example 11–12.

C: V of vi vi   V6/5 of vi vi   vii°6 of vi vi   a: V of VI VI   V2 of VI VI6   vii°6 of VI VI6

CONSECUTIVE SECONDARY DOMINANTS

These chords are sometimes used in succession, and if three or more occur in a definite pattern, a sequence will result. When in succession, each is followed by a dominant seventh chord whose root is a fourth above or a fifth below (thereby maintaining the V to I relationship). Often, in this progression, the fifth is omitted and the root doubled in alternate chords.

Example 11–13.

C: V7 of iii V7 of vi V7 of ii V7 of V V   V7   I

MODULATION

While the secondary dominant is in a sense "borrowed" from another key, its use does not result in a modulation, because here only a single chord or two is used which is foreign, the new tonality is not firmly established, and the harmonic progression returns immediately to the original tonality. Modulation implies a definite change of key with a wider scope and with a feeling of continuation in that new key.

Notwithstanding the above statements, the secondary dominants are sometimes used as pivot chords in modulation, the secondary dominant in the original key being the dominant in the key of destination. After this progression the new key is established in the usual manner by means of an authentic cadence.

Example 11–14.

F: I   IV$^6_4$ I   V–$_7$ vi   ii$_6$ V$_7$ I $\{$V$_7$ of ii
g: $\{$ V$_7$ i   V   i   ii°$_6$ i$^6_4$ V$_7$ i

CROSS RELATION

This term refers to the relationship of a tone in one chord and the same tone or octave appearing in a different voice, chromatically altered, in the next chord. An example would be a G in the soprano followed by a G sharp in the tenor in the next chord. This normally disturbs the flow of the music and hinders smooth voice leading. While cross relation is found in the works of the masters and was successfully used by them, the technique is a delicate one which requires very careful handling. For the present, cross relation will not be permitted, but the note followed by the alteration of that note must appear in the same voice.

Example 11–15.

C: I   V$_7$ of vi   vi   I   V$_7$ of vi   vi

Keyboard Work Involving Secondary Dominants

If two ideas are kept in mind, the playing of these chords in progressions should not be difficult. First, these are chords with a basically dominant structure with which we have already had considerable experience. By being certain that the chord is a V, V_7, or vii_6°, with possible inversions, the structure will be correct. Second, the chord of resolution (unless irregular) should be kept in mind as a temporary tonic; its dominant should then be constructed, finally progressing to the chord of resolution. Always think of the progression V to I in terms of the secondary dominant, knowing that the tonic will be another triad in the given key.

It is essential that the progressions be as smooth as possible and that the altered tone or tones progress stepwise in the same voice.

Example 11–16 indicates possible procedures regarding secondary dominant chords.

Example 11–16.

Writing for Two Voices

By studying examples of two-part writing, either vocal or instrumental, the following points will be observed:

1. The intervals most frequently used in two-part writing are thirds and sixths, because they are consonant intervals and clarify the harmony (major or minor) intended. Perfect fourths and fifths are not used as often, because they have a hollow, empty sound and do not clarify the major–minor element. A triad is major or minor depending on the type of third it contains (or sixth, if inverted), while the fifth will always be perfect.

Augmented fourths and diminished fifths are useful if the interval consists of the fourth and seventh steps of the scale, because these intervals then resolve to sixths and thirds, respectively. The dissonance of this interval stimulates motion.

Seconds and sevenths are used occasionally for color and to produce a desired dissonant effect, and resolve into consonances.

The use of intervals other than the thirds and sixths is determined by the need for variety and interest and by the voice leading. All intervals are selected primarily on the basis of their harmonic implications.

Example 11–17.

2. Octaves and unisons are used as relief from the implied harmony. They are consonant, and a phrase or composition often ends with one or the other. Parallel octaves and unisons are usually avoided as they tend to eliminate the idea of two voices. For variety, a phrase or other section within a composition may be written in octaves or unison, but the purpose here is one of contrast.

3. In vocal writing, the interval between the two voices should rarely exceed an octave, although in instrumental writing the interval spacing of over an octave may be used, often effectively.

4. Non-harmonic tones can be used successfully in two-part writing, for, besides giving melodic interest and individuality to each part, these tones will help develop interesting rhythmic patterns. Parallel motion is good, if this device is not overdone.

Example 11–18.

5. Although the melody is usually in the upper voice, it may be placed with advantage in the lower of the two voices, the harmonic implications then appearing in the upper part. Sometimes, if the upper voice is in free style, a descant will result, which is especially effective in the treble range.

Example 11–19.

Échappée and Cambiata

Both the *échappée* and the *cambiata* are unaccented non-harmonic tones which usually embellish a melodic progression of the interval of a second, either up or down. On occasion they may occur between intervals larger than a second. Both of these non-harmonic tones occur on the weak part of the beat or measure and usually appear in the soprano voice in a downward melodic progression.

The *Échappée,* or "escape tone," is approached stepwise in the direction which is opposite to that of the resolution, then moves by a skip (usually a third) to the note of resolution.

Example 11–20.

The *Cambiata* is, in a sense, the opposite of the *échappée*. It is approached by a downward skip (usually a third) and is resolved stepwise upward. It might be referred to as an unaccented *appoggiatura* because of its approach and resolution. The effect will be completely different because of the difference between the unaccented and accented elements.

Example 11–21.

Assignments

1. Harmonize the following progressions in four-part chorale style:

   (a) Key of C: I–V of vi–vi–V of ii–ii–V–I
   (b) Key of g minor: i–V$_7$ of iv–iv–V$_5^6$ of V–V–V$_5^6$–i
   (c) Key of A: I–V$_7$ of iii–iii–V$_7$ of ii–ii–V$_7$–i
   (d) Key of f minor: i–V$_2$ of VI–VI$_6$–iv–i$_4^6$–V$_5^6$ of V–V–V$_7$–i

2. Listen to progressions involving secondary dominants as they are played and determine the identity of each chord. Write the bass line, then the soprano line, then label the chords.

3. Identify, by hearing only, secondary dominants when played in a progression. Determine which step or steps of the scale are altered and listen to the chord of resolution.

4. Play the progressions which appear in the keyboard section in all keys, thinking each secondary dominant as it is played. Play a succession of secondary dominant seventh chords as described in the section on "Specific Secondary Dominants."

5. Non-pianists: Play original progressions involving secondary dominants, in piano style and in different keys, major and minor. Pianists: Play original progressions involving secondary dominants in free piano style.

6. Sing secondary dominant chords in a given key, using letter names; then sing the chord of resolution.

7. Harmonize the following figured basses in chorale style, using the *échappée* (ech.) and *cambiata* (camb.) where appropriate:

   (a)

(b)

(c)

(d)

8. Harmonize the following soprano melodies, using secondary dominant chords where feasible. Non-harmonic tones are indicated by a plus sign and are to be labeled specifically. Other non-harmonic tones may be added in the other voices.

(e) BACH, Fur deinen Thron tret' ich hiermit (transposed).

(f) KELLER, American Hymn.

9. Write one original exercise in major and one in minor, each including examples of secondary dominants, the *échappée*, and the *cambiata*. (The length is to be determined by the instructor.)

10. Analyze the following excerpts harmonically and stylistically, noting particularly secondary dominant chords and non-harmonic tones.

(a) HANDEL, Sonata in C (*Allegro*).

(b) Johann Krieger, Sarabande, from Partita No. 2 (*Andante con grandessa*).

(c) Schumann, Rondoletto (*Gaiamente*).

(d) Froberger, Suite, "Auff die Mayerin" (from Theme).

(e) SCHUMANN, Northern Song (*In modo popolare*).

(f) SCHUBERT, Impromptu, Op. 142, No. 1 (*Allegro moderato*).

(g) SCHUMANN, Blumenstuck (*Wieder bewegter*).

11. Reduce one or more of the excerpts in assignment 10 to the harmonic rhythm and melodic rhythm patterns. Now write an original work based on the harmonic formula and harmonic rhythm of the original excerpt. Use an original style and melodic rhythm.

12. Write a composition for two voices (vocal or instrumental) in A B A form, each section consisting of at least eight measures.

13. Compose a free composition in any medium, experimenting with secondary dominant chords. (The length of this work is to be determined by the instructor.)

14. Analyze, bring to class, and discuss music being studied which illustrates the use of the secondary dominant chords. Find examples of the *échappée* and the *cambiata*.

12

THE SECONDARY
SEVENTH

The V_7 is the only seventh chord which has been studied up to this point because it has been universally accepted as a basic harmonic sound and has been in constant and frequent usage for several centuries. Of lesser use but still important in the common practice period are the seventh chords built on each of the other degrees of the diatonic scale. These are called secondary seventh chords and are formed by adding the interval of a third to the existing diatonic triad. There are countless examples of these chords in the music of the eighteenth and nineteenth centuries and in our own century in the musical vocabulary of impressionism and the popular music field.

STRUCTURE

These seventh chords are formed on the first, second, third, fourth, sixth, and seventh degrees of the scale. They differ in structure in much the same way as triads on different degrees of the scale. In Example 12–1 the structure of each of the seventh chords in major and minor is illustrated in terms of the type of triad and interval of the seventh included in each. Listen to these to observe the differences in quality and in the degree of dissonance between them.

Example 12–1.

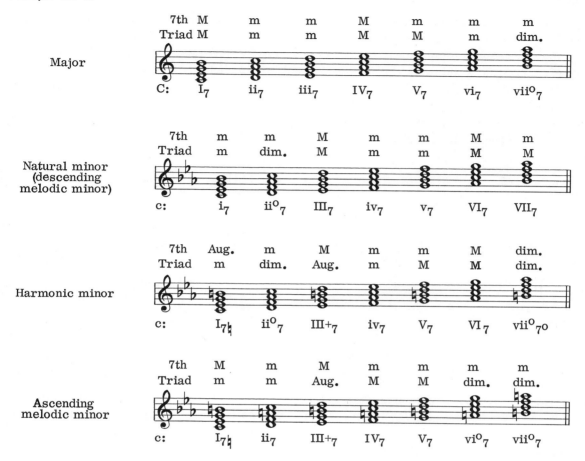

From the above illustration seven different seventh chord structures are formed. These seven types of seventh chords are written in Example 12–2 in order from largest to smallest and beginning on the same note so the differences between them can be readily observed. The type of triad and interval from the root to the seventh is given above the chord; the label below the chord indicates first the triad, then the seventh. The terms in parentheses are those commonly used to identify the particular chord.

Example 12–2.

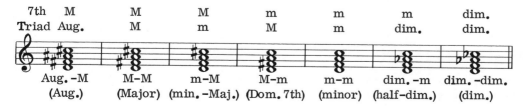

FUNCTION

The general use of secondary seventh chords as independent chords is comparatively recent, although the practice of a seventh being added to the triad in the form of a non-harmonic tone, notably the suspension, was common from the seventeenth century. Later the chord with the seventh became independent and the seventh resolved as a chord tone into the next chord.

In some cases the seventh of a secondary seventh chord may still be considered a non-harmonic tone, such as the suspension, passing tone, or *appoggiatura*, depending on the chord structure and movement of voices. Even the seventh chord itself may be analyzed in several different ways. Context and the specific function of the seventh are the determining factors.

Example 12–3.   BACH, O Herre Gott, dein göttlich Wort.

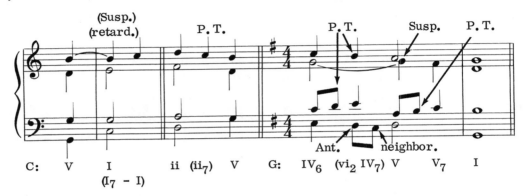

These chords are used to lend color and variety to the harmonic texture of the music, to give fuller, richer sound to a progression because of the addition of the seventh, and to suggest more harmonic possibilities to the harmonization of a melody. Avoid the overuse of these chords, as too much color and variety will lessen their effectiveness.

Example 12–4. BACH, Nun ruhen alle Walder.

DOUBLING

Secondary seventh chords may occur either as complete chords, with all four tones being present, as in the Bach excerpt above, or as incomplete chords. The advantage of the complete chord is the fullness of sound which is created, while the advantage of the incomplete chord is that the essence of the seventh chord is retained without the richness of the complete chord. In the incomplete seventh chord the root is usually doubled, the seventh is often placed in the soprano voice, and most often the fifth of the chord is omitted. The use of one or the other of these chord structures might be compared to the complete and incomplete V_7 chord.

Example 12–5.

C: ii₇   V - ₇   I   ii₇   V - ₇   I
(Inc.) (Complete)   (Complete) (Inc.)

The vii°₇ should be written as a complete chord except when the resolution is to iii, in which case the root may be doubled. This is an exception to the rule never to double the leading tone. If one seventh chord progresses to a different seventh chord, whether a sequence results or not, one of the two will normally be complete and the other incomplete.

Example 12–6.

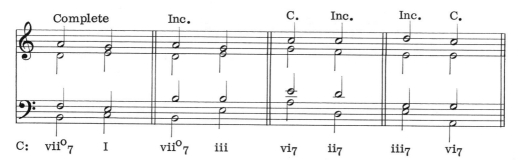

C: vii°₇   I   vii°₇   iii   vi₇   ii₇   iii₇   vi₇

HARMONIC APPROACH

The principles involving good chord progression, as discussed in Chapter 9, are as valid in the use of seventh chords as they are in the use of triads. Thus, a progression which would be effective in approaching the ii chord would be equally effective in approaching the ii₇, realizing the difference in quality caused by the added seventh.

Example 12–7.

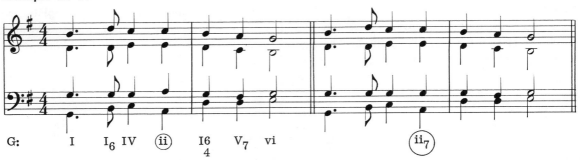

The seventh in the secondary seventh chords may be approached with or without preparation, depending on the effect desired. This aspect has been discussed in Chapter 8 in regard to the V_7 chord. Context and the type of voice movement are the determining factors. The illustration in Example 12–8 shows first the seventh of the chord which is prepared and then the seventh of the chord which is not prepared.

Example 12–8.

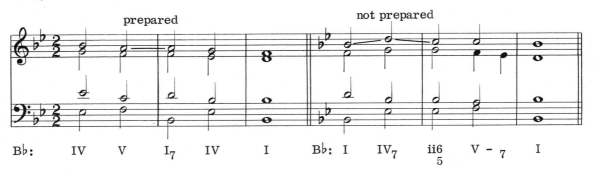

RESOLUTION

The normal resolution of these chords is to a chord a perfect fourth up or a perfect fifth down, in keeping with the basic harmonic progression, the V–I principle. In this progression the seventh resolves down one step, the fifth down a step, the third may either resolve down the interval of a third or up one step, and the root will move up a fourth or down a fifth. While this is for the seventh chord in root position, the same principle applies to the inversion of seventh chords, although here the root remains on the same tone to become the fifth of the following chord of resolution. The voice leading, in other words, follows the regular resolution of the V_7.

Example 12–9.

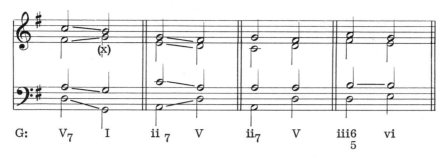

G: V₇ I ii₇ V ii₇ V iii⁶₅ vi

Another possibility is that of the seventh chord assuming the role of a dependent chord, in which the chord seventh is formed by a suspension or an *appoggiatura*. In this progression the chord seventh resolves down one step and the other tones remain stationary. A different seventh chord in a different position is formed, the root of the chord of resolution being a third below the root of the original seventh chord. This progression is especially valuable in resolving the IV₇ in major or minor and the VI₇ in minor, as their normal resolution to a chord a perfect fourth above would result in a chord foreign to the key itself.

Example 12–10.

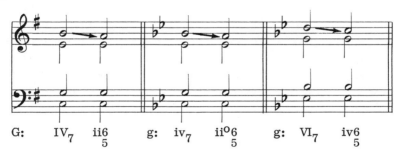

G: IV₇ ii⁶₅   g: iv₇ ii°⁶₅   g: VI₇ iv⁶₅

Secondary seventh chords may also resolve to other seventh chords in a sequential pattern, progressing up a perfect fourth. They may also progress to other positions and inversions of the same chord, this being movement but not actually constituting a resolution.

Example 12–11.

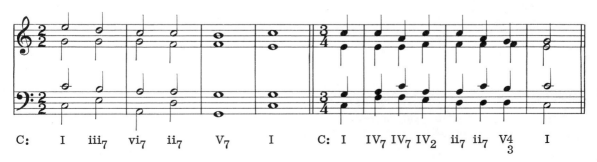

C: I iii₇ vi₇ ii₇ V₇ I   C: I IV₇ IV₇ IV₂ ii₇ ii₇ V⁴₃ I

INVERSION

Secondary seventh chords are found in root position and in all inversions. They appear most frequently in root position with the first inversion next in preference. The second and third inversions are used effectively where a specific quality and bass movement are demanded. Tones are not usually doubled or omitted in the inversions.

Example 12–12.

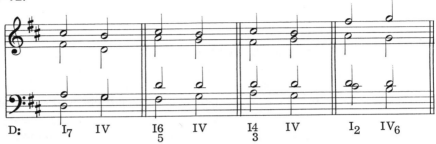

PARALLEL FIFTHS

Although the use of parallel fifths will continue to be avoided, there are instances in the use of secondary seventh chords in which parallel fifths may be allowed for more natural voice leading. This problem arises particularly in the use of these chords, because in the major seventh chord and in the minor seventh chord there are two pairs of perfect fifths. The richness of the sound of these seventh chords, however, overcomes the hollow sound of the parallel fifths. These fifths can be avoided by inverting the interval of the fifth, or can be somewhat obscured by the use of a suspension in the chord of resolution.

Example 12–13.

MODULATION

These chords may be used successfully as pivot chords in modulation because they are not of a dominant nature, except the vii°_{7}, and so do not determine the key. The choice of keys is limited, but the quality of the individual chord makes it an effective pivot chord device.

Example 12–14.

Eb: I   V4   I6   {ii7
                3   Ab:{vi7   ii   V7   I   f#:   i   V7   i   {VI7
                                                                              A:{IV7   ii°6   V7   I
                                                                                              5

Principles Involving Specific Seventh Chords

We shall discuss now each of the secondary seventh chords, including the characteristics and peculiarities of each. The diminished seventh chord, which requires more extended study, will be discussed in Chapter 13. Following the discussion is a table giving the chord of preparation, the seventh chord, and the regular and irregular resolutions of each.

TONIC SEVENTH

This chord is effective in major keys because of the bright sound of the major triad plus a major seventh and because it is an active form of the I chord. When used in the minor mode the seventh is lowered so that its resolution will be down a major second (descending melodic minor scale), rather than the unnatural sound of an augmented second as caused by the use of the harmonic form of the minor. The I_7 is used successfully as either a dependent chord (the seventh serving as a suspension or *appoggiatura*) or as an independent chord.

Example 12–15.

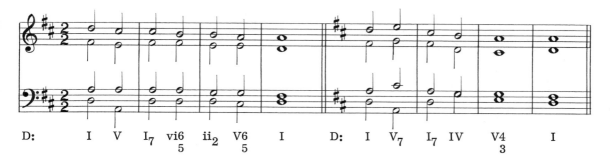

D: I   V   I7   vi6   ii2   V6   I   D: I   V7   I7   IV   V4   I
                       5   5   3

Example 12–16. SCHUMANN, Spring Song, from "Album for the Young."

SUPERTONIC SEVENTH

This is the most widely used of all secondary seventh chords and is found most often in the first inversion (ii_5^6). Although it may occur anywhere in the phrase as a substitute for ii, its main function is that of a dominant preparation in a cadence, following the IV and preceding the I_4^6 or the V. The ii_7 is equally effective in major and minor. In Chapter 15 we will discover the use of the half-diminished form (found now in minor keys) in major keys.

Example 12–17.

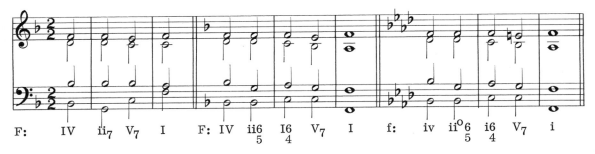

In Example 12–18, the resolution to the dominant is delayed by means of a secondary dominant and a $^6_4$ chord.

Example 12–18. SCHUMANN, The Poet Speaks, from "Scenes of Childhood."

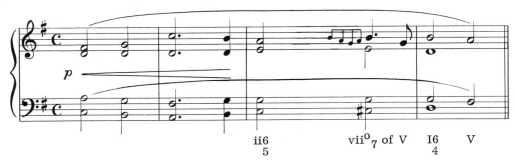

MEDIANT SEVENTH

The normal resolution is to the vi, although it sometimes resolves to IV. In major keys the chord is usually complete, but when it is incomplete, the third is doubled and the fifth omitted. In minor keys, for better voice leading, the fifth ascends when it is the raised leading tone and it descends when it is lowered seventh scale degree.

Example 12-19.

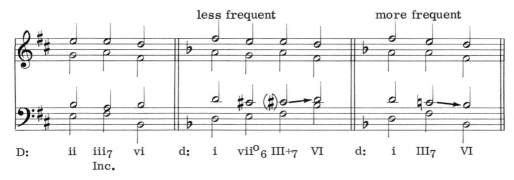

SUBDOMINANT SEVENTH

This chord is similar to the I_7 because, besides being based on a primary triad, it has the same chord structure as I_7 in both major and minor keys. It is different, however, in that the normal resolution is not to a chord a perfect fifth below, which would be vii_7°, but rather to a form of ii_7. The exception to this is when it is found in a sequence. In the progression to a form of ii_7, the seventh of the IV_7 is the only tone that moves and serves as a suspension or an *appoggiatura* in resolving to a ii_5^6, thus making it a dependent chord. Another typical resolution is to I_4^6 or V_7 in a cadential pattern.

Example 12-20.

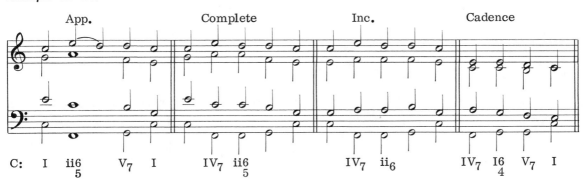

Example 12–21. BEETHOVEN, Sonata, Op. 10, No. 2 (*Allegretto*).

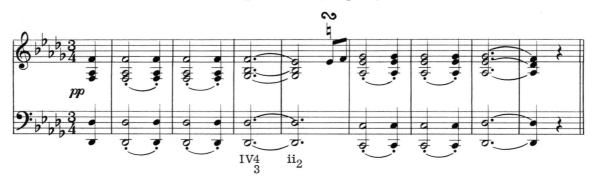

SUBMEDIANT SEVENTH

This chord creates more interest and urgency in minor keys than in major because of its structure. In major it is actually a tonic chord with a sixth added and contains the minor seventh as the characteristic interval, whereas in minor the structure is that of a major triad with a major seventh added (a major seventh chord). The resolution is to ii or ii$_7$, with the ii$_7^\circ$ being more frequent in minor keys because the rather thin sound of the diminished triad on ii° in minor does not produce the interest usually desired.

Example 12–22.

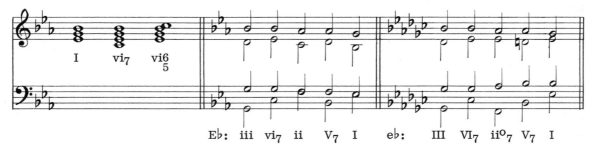

In Example 12–23, the resolution, while based on the second scale step, is actually a secondary dominant seventh chord.

Example 12–23. BEETHOVEN, Sonata, Op. 2, No. 3 (*Allegro con brio*).

LEADING TONE SEVENTH

The diminished seventh chord (vii°$_7$° in minor) is the subject of the following chapter; this discussion deals with the half-diminished seventh chord (vii°$_7$ in major) and the dominant seventh chord (VII$_7$ in minor, using the natural minor form). The vii°$_7$ in major usually assumes its dominant role and resolves to I, in which the diminished fifth interval, characteristic of the V$_7$, contracts to form a third. This chord is sometimes referred to as an incomplete V$_9$ chord (V$_9$ without a root), but the label of vii°$_7$ more clearly defines the chord and avoids confusion later. The other function of vii°$_7$ in major is to resolve down a perfect fifth to iii. This is most useful in sequential patterns.

Example 12–24.

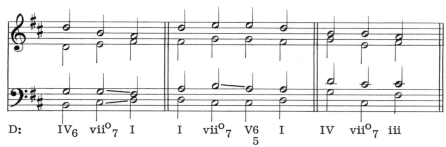

Example 12–25. Schubert, Sonata, Op. 120 (2nd movement).

In minor keys, this chord is often used with the lowered leading tone, thus producing a seventh chord with a V$_7$ structure. This chord resolves to III, suggesting a possible modulation to the relative major key, and is effective in injecting a major feeling in the minor mode. It may be considered a secondary dominant because of its structure, but as there are no accidentals, the chord remains within the key.

Example 12–26.

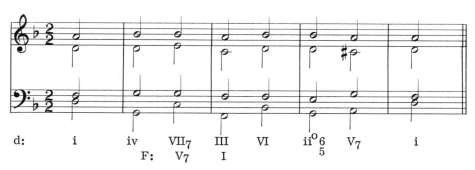

Table of Secondary Seventh Chords

The table below represents a brief summary of chord progressions involving secondary seventh chords. It does not show all possibilities, but rather those which are most frequently used. No indication as to the actual structure of the individual chords is given (type of Roman numeral), as this would be different for each mode. Chords are indicated below in root position, although inversions of all chords, including the secondary seventh chords, are possible and useful.

Chord of Preparation	Secondary Seventh Chord	Regular Resolution	Irregular Resolution
V, V$_7$ or I	I$_7$	IV	II$_7$ or VI$_7$
IV, II, VI or I	II$_7$	V or I	I, III or VI
I, II, III or VII	III$_7$	VI	IV, II or I
I, IV or VI	IV$_7$	II$_7$ or V	I or II
III or I	VI$_7$	II	IV or V
IV or I	VII$_7$	I or III	V$_7$

Keyboard Work Using Secondary Seventh Chords

For practice purposes, the sequential pattern is useful in playing progressions including secondary seventh chords. Different patterns may be devised, but Example 12–27 illustrates several possibilities. Note that illustration B is the minor key version of illustration A and that C and D represent the initial patterns which can be continued. All of these should be played in both major and minor keys.

Example 12–27.

Writing for Three Treble Voices

Because treble voices, both instrumental and vocal, are lighter by themselves than when supported by lower voices, and because the range in vocal music is not as great, certain principles must be considered for three-part treble writing. In writing for three treble instruments, remember that the range is wider and there is more freedom of motion.

CHORD STRUCTURE

The complete chord is possible when triads and their inversions are used. When using seventh chords or incomplete triads, follow the general principles of four-part writing for omitting and doubling tones.

Example 12–28.

MOVEMENT OF PARTS

In general, close position is more effective than open, although open is often used. Contrary motion is not as essential here as in four-part harmony and the overlapping of voices is often used to good advantage. Parallel motion of all voices is effective in the treble due to the range and quality of tone in that register.

Use non-harmonic tones to stimulate movement and for variety. It is usually advisable to begin with basic harmony and then elaborate with secondary chords and non-harmonic tones.

Example 12–29.

CHORD ARRANGEMENT

Inversions are especially useful in three-part writing and are used in place of many root position chords, even at the end of a phrase, because of their natural lightness of texture. The use of parallel thirds and sixths is as effective here as in two-part writing. In a cadence a vii_6° can sometimes be substituted for a V_7 with good effect. Also, a unison or an octave at the end of a phrase or composition sounds well.

Example 12–30.

$$\text{IV}_6 \quad V_7 \quad \text{I}_4^6 \quad \text{vi} \quad \text{ii}_6 \quad \text{vii}^\circ{}_6 \quad \text{I}_6$$

FREE STYLE

All three parts need not be sounded at all times, but each may enter separately or drop out momentarily. Context and texture will be the determining factors here.

Example 12–31. MENDELSSOHN, Lift Thine Eyes.

Assignments

1. Harmonize each of the following progressions in four-part chorale style:

    (a) Key of C: $\text{I}–\text{I}_7–\text{IV}–\text{ii}_7–\text{I}_4^6–\text{V}_7–\text{I}$
    (b) Key of d minor: $\text{i}–\text{vii}_6–\text{III}_7–\text{VI}–\text{iv}_7–\text{ii}^\circ{}_5^6–\text{V}_7–\text{i}$
    (c) Key of A flat: $\text{I}–\text{IV}_7–\text{ii}_5^6–\text{V}–\text{I}_3^4–\text{V}_7–\text{I}$
    (d) Key of e minor: $\text{i}–\text{VI}_5^6–\text{iv}–\text{iv}_2–\text{ii}^\circ–\text{V}_7–\text{i}$

2. Listen to progressions involving secondary seventh chords as they are played and determine the identity of each chord. Write the bass line, then the soprano line, then label the chords. When these chords can be heard easily, identify them, by hearing only, when played in a progression.

3. Play the progressions which appear in the keyboard section in all major and minor keys, determining each secondary seventh chord and position as it is played.

4. Non-pianists: Play original progressions and sequences involving these chords in piano style and in different major and minor keys. Pianists: Play the same in free piano style.

5. Sing secondary seventh chords in root position and in any inversion in a given key, using letter names.

6. Harmonize the following figured basses in chorale style, using non-harmonic tones:

(a)

(b)

(c)

(d)

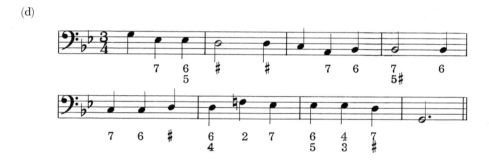

7. Harmonize the following soprano melodies, using secondary seventh chords and non-harmonic tones:

(a)

(b)

(c)

(d) BACH, Du Friedensfurst, Herr Jesu Christ.

(e) ENGLISH, Drink To Me Only With Thine Eyes.

8. Harmonize folk songs or other familiar tunes in either piano or chorale style, employing secondary seventh chords.

9. Write short original exercises in major and minor, using examples of secondary seventh chords.

10. Analyze the following excerpts harmonically and stylistically, noting the function of the secondary seventh chords in each example:

(a) BEETHOVEN, Sonata, Op. 27, No. 2 (*Adagio sostenuto*).

(b) SCHUMANN, Album for the Young, No. 30.

(c) SCHUMANN, Child Falling Asleep, from "Scenes of Childhood."

(d) HAYDN, Sonata in E flat (*Allegro moderato*).

(e) BEETHOVEN, Sonata, Op. 28 (*Andante*).

(f) Rachmaninoff, Moment Musical, Op. 16, No. 3.

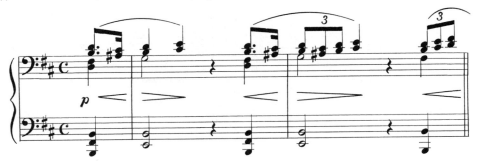

(g) Beethoven, Sonata, Op. 10, No. 3 (*Presto*).

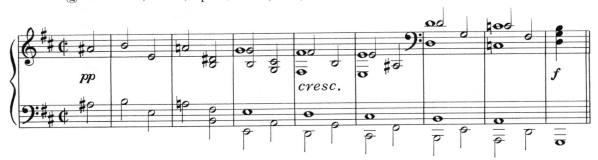

(h) Brahms, Intermezzo, Op. 118, No. 2.

(i) Grieg, Ballade, Op. 24—Variation No. 9 (two excerpts).

(j) PINTO, Tom Thumb's March.

(k) MELLISH–QUILTER, Drink To Me Only With Thine Eyes.

in the cup and I'll not ask for wine

11. Analyze the following excerpt harmonically and stylistically and comment on the adaptation of the principles of three-part treble writing as presented in this chapter.

MENDELSSOHN, Lift Thine Eyes.

12. Write a three-part treble setting of a familiar melody. Harmonize the following soprano melody for three treble voices:

13. Write a free composition in any medium, employing secondary seventh chords. (The length of this work is to be determined by the instructor.)

14. Analyze, bring to class, and discuss music in which secondary seventh chords are present.

15. Analyze the harmony of the popular songs, "Tea for Two," "Talk of the Town," or another song using secondary seventh chords extensively. Play it for keyboard work in any key.

13

THE DIMINISHED SEVENTH

This chord, which was frequently used for color and for unstable warmth from the common practice period up to our own time, is formed by a succession of minor thirds. This construction divides the octave into four equal parts. In keeping with the analysis of the other seventh chords discussed in Chapter 12, this seventh chord consists of a diminished triad and a diminished seventh (see discussion on page 163). The diminished seventh chord as a diatonic chord is found only on the leading tone in minor keys. This same chord, however, may be used as the leading tone seventh chord in major keys as well, providing the chord seventh is chromatically lowered.

Example 13-1.

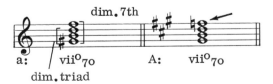

The reasons for discussing this chord apart from the other seventh chords are threefold:

1. The presence of the fourth and seventh scale steps implies that it is derived from the V chord, and, while the vii$_7^\circ$ in major (with a minor seventh) has the same scale degrees present, the lowered seventh of the diminished seventh chord presents more possibilities for use.

2. Because it is the only secondary seventh chord with a dominant derivation, it may be successfully used as a secondary dominant.

3. Because of its ambiguity (discussed later), the diminished seventh chord is very useful for purposes of modulation.

CHARACTERISTICS

First compare the sound of the diminished seventh chord with that of the other seventh chords studied thus far. Now listen to the sound of the diminished seventh chord and to the inversions of the same chord. Notice that the root position chord and the inversions have the same harmonic sound and tension, despite the fact that the bass note is different in each case. Because all tones are equidistant, the above similarity of sound is possible. This is a dissonant seventh chord made up entirely of active tones and including two interlocking pairs of diminished fifths. Despite this construction, the sound of the chord is not as harsh as one might expect.

Example 13–2.

This chord is often referred to as an incomplete V_9 chord, that is, a V_9 without a root. While we will not use this terminology, the connection between the diminished seventh chord and its dominant derivation can be clearly realized in its use.

Example 13–3.

It is sometimes used as a substitute for the V chord or the V_7 in situations where more color or a different quality is desired. Because the chord seventh is the sixth scale step, a new and refreshing harmonization with a dominant flavor is possible for this tone.

Example 13–4.

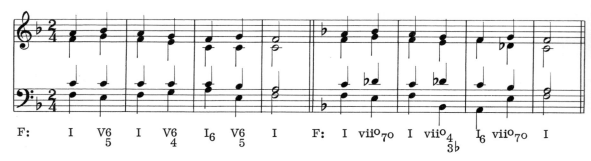

The vii°$_7$° chord originally consisted of a V$_5^6$ chord with a suspension or an *appoggiatura* resolving to the root of the chord. Later it became an independent chord with individual root movement.

Example 13–5. BACH, Christ, der du bist der helle Tag.

dm: vii°$_7$°V$_6$ i

PREPARATION

The seventh of the diminished seventh chord is approached in the same manner as that of the other secondary seventh chords: by preparation, by step, or by skip. The other three tones of the chord are approached as smoothly as possible with good voice leading.

Being derived from the dominant, the chord of preparation is the same as that of the dominant chord.

Example 13–6.

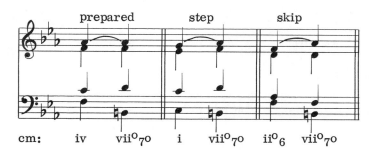

cm: iv   vii°$_7$°   i   vii°$_7$°   ii°$_6$ vii°$_7$°

DOUBLING AND CHORD STRUCTURE

In four-part harmony, the diminished seventh chord, whether in root position or in an inversion, is used as a complete chord with no tone doubled. All four tones are essential to produce the characteristic sound of the chord. In three-part writing this chord appears as an incomplete seventh chord. As to arrangement of tones in four-part chorale style or in free style, any chord tone may appear in the soprano voice, the choice depending on the melodic line and voice leading. The chord sounds equally well in close or open position.

Example 13–7.

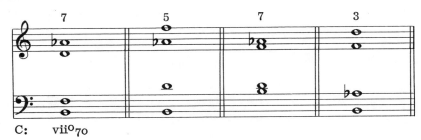

C: vii°7o

RESOLUTION

The normal resolution of the diminished seventh chord in both the major and minor mode is to the tonic chord, because of the natural tendency of the leading tone to resolve to the tonic tone. In this resolution each of the diminished fifth intervals resolves to a third, resulting in a I with doubled third. Each tone resolves stepwise, the fifth and seventh downward and the root and third upward.

Example 13–8.   BACH, Puer natus in Bethlehem.

c: vii°7o i   C: vii°7o I   a: vii°7o i

If the seventh of the chord is placed below the third of the chord, the third may then move down to the root of the I chord. In this instance the parallel fifths in question will have been inverted to form fourths and the resulting irregular voice leading is permissible.

Example 13–9.

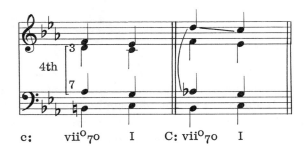

c: vii°7o   I   C: vii°7o   I

Example 13–10. BACH, Herzliebster Jesu, was hast du.

Other possible resolutions of the vii°$_7$° chord are to an inversion of V$_7$ and to a form of IV. In the resolution to a form of V$_7$, the seventh of the vii°$_7$° is actually a non-harmonic tone, making the chord itself a dependent chord. The seventh of the vii°$_7$° may be unresolved in moving to a form of IV.

Example 13–11.

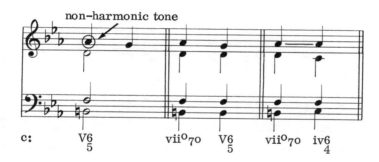

INVERSIONS

The inversions of the vii°$_7$° chord are used frequently, although the third inversion is not as common as the others. The treatment and voice leading are the same as the normal progression of the same chord in root position.

Example 13–12.

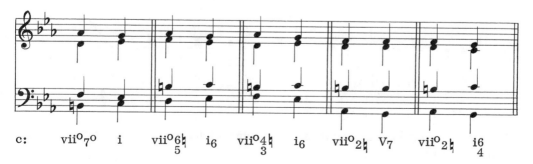

The vii°$^6_5$ is usually preceded by I or ii and resolves to I$_6$.

Example 13–13.

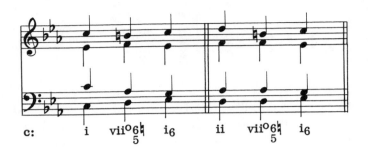

c: i   vii°$^6_5$♮   i$_6$ ii   vii°$^6_5$♮   i$_6$

The vii°$^4_3$ is usually preceded by IV or ii and may resolve to I$_6$, I, or vi$_6$.

Example 13–14.

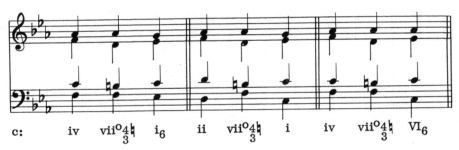

c: iv   vii°$^4_3$♮   i$_6$ ii   vii°$^4_3$♮   i   iv   vii°$^4_3$♮   VI$_6$

The vii°$_2$ is not often used, but when used is preceded by IV$_6$ and resolves to I$^6_4$ or V$_7$ (here the chord seventh produces the effect of a non-harmonic tone).

Example 13–15.

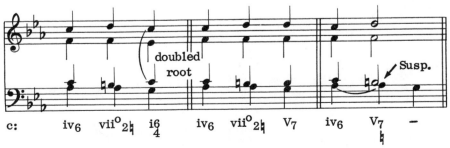

c: iv$_6$ vii°$_2$♮   i$^6_4$ iv$_6$ vii°$_2$♮   V$_7$ iv$_6$ V$_7$ —

A vii°$_{7°}$ in root position or in an inversion is sometimes followed by the same chord in other inversions or in root position.

Example 13-16.

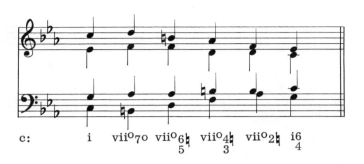

c: i   vii°7o vii°6♮ vii°4♮ vii°2♮ i6
                          5   3   4

vii°7o AS SECONDARY DOMINANT

These chords are very effective as secondary dominants because of their dominant derivation and chord or resolution and because they produce more chromatic sound and movement than the V_7 itself.

When used as secondary dominants, they will always resolve to their own tonic triads, which may be major or minor, depending on the natural structure of the chord of resolution.

Example 13-17.

A: I   vii°7o vi   vii°7o iii   vii°7oii ii6   vii°7o IV   vii°7o   V   I   -
           of   of   of   of   of
           VI   iii   ii   IV   V

vii°7o IN MODULATION

Because any of the four tones in the chord may serve as a leading tone, the vii°7o is useful as a modulating device. This chord will sound the same, regardless of which of the four tones is to be used as the leading tone, but the notation will differ. Enharmonic changes in notation will be necessary to create a logical progression from the diminished seventh chord to its chord of resolution in the new key. In this modulation the vii°7o becomes an enharmonic pivot chord.

Example 13–18.

The chord of resolution will indicate in sound that a modulation has taken place if the establishment of the new key follows, or it will indicate that the seventh chord is simply a secondary dominant if the shift of key is temporary and the return to the original key is immediate.

There are three possible diminished seventh chords in music, the ones built on C, C sharp, and D, all others being the enharmonic equivalent of these three. In Example 13–19 the diminished seventh chord resolves to its major tonic. Each, however, may resolve to its own minor tonic just as easily.

Example 13–19.

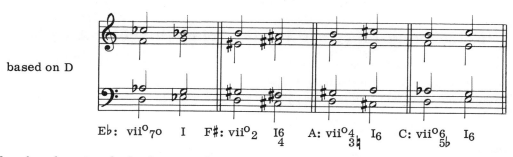

based on D

Eb: vii°7o   I   F#: vii°2   I6/4   A: vii°4/3♮   I6   C: vii°6/5b   I6

Therefore, by using the leading tone diminished seventh chord in a given key plus the other two vii°7o chords as secondary dominants, it is possible to modulate from one key to *any other* key by using the vii°7o chord as a pivot chord.

The use of the vii°7o of the new key as the pivot chord in modulation might not always be advisable because the new key is then reached too quickly. This chord, however, is very satisfactory for a rapid change of key. Also, the chord of resolution of the vii°7o may be a better pivot chord than the vii°7o itself, the vii°7o here acting as a stimulus to the change of key.

Pedal Point

This non-harmonic tone, sometimes referred to as *organ point*, consists of a note, usually in the bass, which is held through several harmonic changes and is heard against these changes of harmony. One of the most natural forms of dissonance, pedal point may be held for a measure or two, but usually is held for a longer duration. The most frequently used tones for the pedal point are the tonic and dominant, and sometimes the subdominant.

Example 13-20.

C: I   iii   IV   V   I
I ——————————————

Example 13-21. SCHUMANN, Carnaval—Valse Allemande.

Molto vivace

pp

Ped. ————————

Neighboring Tones and Passing Tones (Irregular Aspects)

Two neighboring tones may be combined in a single ornament while still maintaining their original function (see the first illustration in Example 13–22). A neighboring tone may be preceded or followed by a non-harmonic tone adjacent to it (see the second illustration).

Example 13–22.

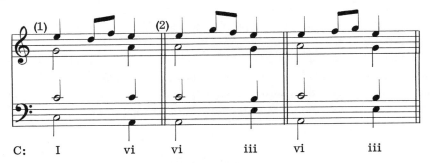

An irregular approach to an unaccented passing tone is by a skip, usually an interval of a third. This is contrary to the stepwise procedure studied earlier, but the passing tone function is now implied and the passing tone itself resolves stepwise in the same direction.

Example 13–23.

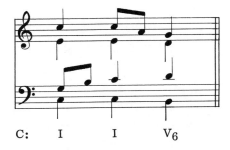

Assignments

1. Harmonize each of the following progressions in four-part chorale style:

    (a) Key of g minor: i–V$_5^6$–i–vii°$_{7°}$–i–ii°$_5^6$–V$_7$–i
    (b) Key of E flat: I–vii°$_{7°}$–I–V–vii°$_{7°}$ of V–V–V$_7$–I
    (c) Key of d minor: i–iv–vii°$_3^4$–i$_6$–vii°$_5^6$–vii°$_{7°}$–i
    (d) Key of G: I–vii°$_{7°}$–V$_5^6$–V$_2$ of IV–IV$_6$–vii°$_2$–I$_4^6$–V$_7$–I

2. Listen to progressions, including phrases of actual music, which have diminished seventh chords, and determine as they are played the identity of each chord, as in previous chapters.

3. At the keyboard, play and memorize the following progressions. Then play progression (a) in all minor keys and progression (b) in all major keys.

(a)

(b)

4. Non-pianists: Play original progressions involving diminished seventh chords (as vii°$_7$° in the original key and also as secondary dominants) in piano style and in major and minor keys. Pianists: Play the same but in free piano style.

5. Write each of the following diminished seventh chords in four ways in minor and in four ways in major by the use of enharmonic notation. Resolve each as a vii°$_7$° chord to its own tonic chord.

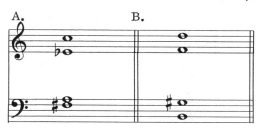

6. Play any diminished seventh chord and resolve it into four different major and minor keys, using each tone in the chord successively as the leading tone, resolving into its own tonic chord.

7. Sing diminished seventh chords. Sing, by letter names, four different interpretations of the same chord.

8. Harmonize the following figured basses in chorale style, using non-harmonic tones:

(a)

(b)

(c)

(d)

9. Harmonize the following soprano melodies, using the vii°$_7$° chord where indicated and wherever else it seems appropriate. Also use non-harmonic tones, particularly those discussed in this chapter.

(a)

(b)

(c)

(d)

(e)

10. Write a twenty-four-measure work in piano style which modulates from D to A flat and back to D, using diminished seventh chords as pivot chords.

11. Harmonize folk songs or other familiar tunes at the keyboard in piano style, using vii°$_7$° chords.

12. Write short original exercises in major and minor, using examples of diminished seventh chords.

13. Analyze the following excerpts harmonically and stylistically, noting the diminished seventh chord and its function in each example:

(a) HELLER, Curious Story.

(b) BEETHOVEN, Sonata, Op. 13 (1st movement) (*Adagio*).

(c) DEBUSSY, Clair de lune.

(d) BEETHOVEN, Sonata, Op. 49, No. 1 (*Rondo*).

(e) SCHUMANN, First Loss, from "Album for the Young."

(f) MENDELSSOHN, Song Without Words, Op. 19, No. 2 (*Andantino espressivo*).

(g) BEETHOVEN, Sonata, Op. 53 (1st movement) (*Allegro con brio*).

(h) Mozart, Sonata in E flat (K282) (*Menuetto*).

(i) Bach, Prelude in C (W. T. C. Book 1).

(j) Brahms, Intermezzo, Op. 76, No. 7.

(k) BACH, Little Prelude in d minor (two excerpts).

final 4 measures.

14. Write a free composition in any medium, employing diminished seventh chords, the pedal point, and the irregular aspects of the neighboring tone and passing tone. (The length of this work is to be determined by the instructor.)

15. Analyze, bring to class, and discuss music in which the above chords and elements appear.

14

CHORDS OF THE NINTH, ELEVENTH, AND THIRTEENTH

We now turn to a group of chords which, for the first time in our study, consist of more than four tones in their complete form. These are formed by the addition of one, two, or three intervals of a third above the seventh of a seventh chord. They are dissonant, have a more complex nature, and should be used sparingly to be most effective. Previously one of the conditions in chord structure was that of doubling, but here the type of chord structure demands the omission of tones which are not essential in traditional four-part harmony.

Example 14–1.

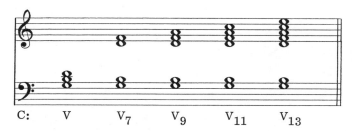

$$C: \quad V \quad V_7 \quad V_9 \quad V_{11} \quad V_{13}$$

Historically, these chords as independent sounds are comparatively recent, being found in music generally from the nineteenth century. They were used much earlier as seventh chords (usually V_7) with non-harmonic tones which then resolved into the parent harmony.

Example 14–2. BACH, Capriccio—Part 3.

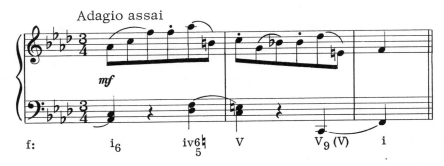

The Ninth Chord

This is the most frequently used of the three chords presented in this chapter and is characterized by a rich, sweet quality. Although it may occur on different steps of the scale, as will be mentioned later, the V_9 is the only one in general usage, and this in both the major and the minor modes.

STRUCTURE

Because of the presence of five tones in the V_9 chord, an unessential tone is omitted in four-part harmony, this tone usually being the fifth of the chord. The exception to this is discussed below in the section on "Resolution." To produce the effect of the ninth, the interval of the ninth is placed in the soprano voice. If it appears in an inner voice, the effect of the chord is less definite but still satisfactory.

There should be at least an interval of a ninth between the root and the ninth (not a second); there may be an interval of a ninth between two adjacent voices. This marks the first departure from the strict principle of not having more than an octave between any of the upper voices in strict writing.

Example 14–3.

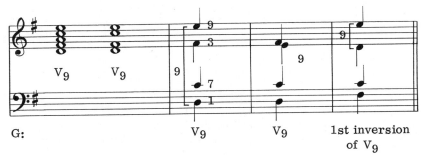

HARMONIC APPROACH

The approach to the V_9 is very similar to that of the V_7, the only new element being the ninth. The V_9 may be preceded by the same chord that precedes the V_7; it may also be preceded by the V_7 which, although basically the same chord, produces enough interest to be effective.

The interval of the ninth may be approached by preparation, by step, or by skip, the manner of approaching it determining the degree of independence of that tone and the chord.

Example 14–4.

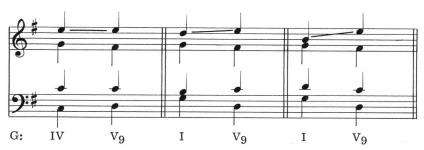

RESOLUTION

When the V_9 occurs as a dependent chord, the ninth may serve as an accented non-harmonic tone and resolve down one step into the root of the resulting V_7. This is the original use of the chord, and in this progression the ninth is the only tone that moves. In the Beethoven excerpt in Example 14–5, both the IV_7 and the V_9 are formed as the result of suspensions in the soprano voice.

Example 14–5. BEETHOVEN, Bagatelle, Op. 119, No. 1 (*Allegretto*).

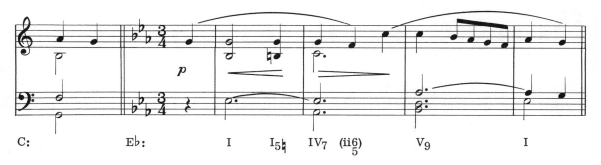

In its regular resolution to I, the voice leading is that of the V_7, with the ninth resolving down one step into the fifth of the tonic triad. In major and in minor (using the ascending melodic minor scale) the ninth may resolve up a step to the leading tone. In this progression the V_9 appears with a fifth but with no third so the V_7, created by the leading tone, will be a complete chord. The resolution here is also to the tonic triad.

Example 14–6.

The chord ninth may skip into a tone in the dominant harmony before resolving to I, and the V_9 may resolve irregularly to the VI or the IV_6. The movement of the ninth determines the effect of the progression.

Example 14–7.

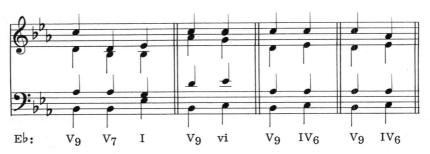

Example 14–8. SCHUBERT, Waltz.

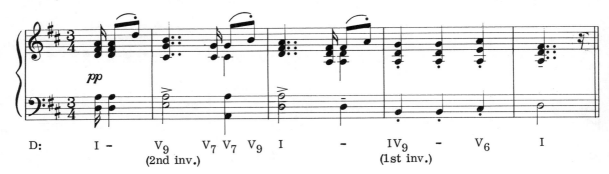

INVERSIONS

The V_9, while found in root position in the great majority of cases, may be used in the first and third inversions in four-part harmony. The second inversion is normally not possible, as the fifth of the chord is usually omitted. The fourth inversion, with the ninth in the bass, is not practical, as the ninth would strongly suggest a non-harmonic tone and the distribution of voices with the ninth below the root would not be recommended.

Example 14–9.

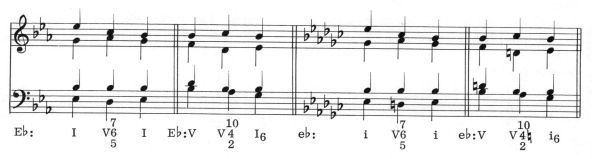

Example 14–10. SCHUMANN, A Curious Story, Op. 15, No. 2.

AS SECONDARY DOMINANTS

The V_9 is effective as a secondary dominant chord, the principles for secondary dominant triads and seventh chords being applicable here as well. The chord of resolution will normally be to a chord whose root is a fifth below, although irregular resolutions are sometimes possible. If the normal chord of resolution is minor, the ninth of the ninth chord should be minor also.

Example 14–11.

OTHER NINTH CHORDS

While nearly all ninth chords in general use are V_9 chords, some examples may be found of ninth chords based on other steps of the scale, notably the ii_9. These are constructed, approached, and resolved in the same manner as the V_9 with different harmonic results due to the different intervallic structure.

Listen to the examples below to determine the effectiveness of the various secondary ninth chords. Also listen to IV_9 in the section on "Resolution."

Example 14–12.

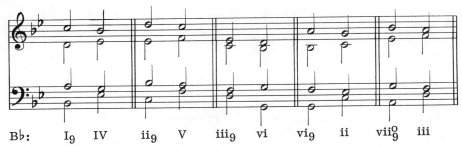

Bb: I_9 IV ii_9 V iii_9 vi vi_9 ii vii^o_9 iii

Eleventh Chords

These chords, limited in their use as independent chords, are actually superimposed chords in which a triad or seventh chord is sounded over a pedal point. In effect the eleventh chord is formed by means of an *appoggiatura*, suspension, or anticipation and is most striking when the eleventh is in the soprano voice. The only eleventh chords in general use are the I_{11} and the V_{11}.

TONIC ELEVENTH CHORD

This chord has two possible structures, that of V_7 over a tonic bass (V_7/I) or vii^o over a tonic bass (vii^o/I). The incomplete V_7 or the vii^o over I automatically eliminates the problem of which tones of the six-note chord to omit. In other words, the third *and* either the fifth or ninth are omitted in this eleventh chord. The resolution is to I.

Example 14–13.

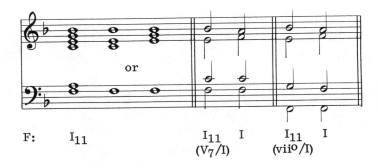

F: I_{11} I_{11} I I_{11} I
                                   (V_7/I)   (vii^o/I)

Example 14–14. TCHAIKOWSKY, Italian Song, Op. 39, No. 15.

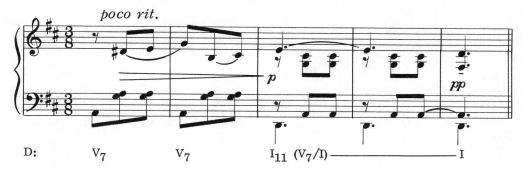

D: V_7 V_7 I_{11} (V_7/I) ——————— I

DOMINANT ELEVENTH CHORD

This chord also has two possible structures, the IV over V (IV/V) or ii_7 over V (ii_7/V). Notice in Example 14–15 that the resolution is either to I or to V_7.

Example 14–15.

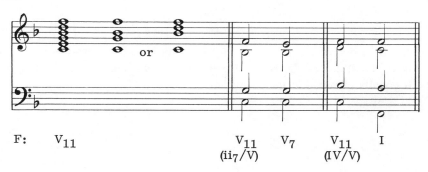

F: V_{11} V_{11} V_7 V_{11} I
                                  (ii_7/V) (IV/V)

Thirteenth Chords

The only practical thirteenth chord is the V_{13}. It may be used as a dependent chord, a V_7 with a non-harmonic tone added which resolves to the fifth of the V_7 chord, or it may be used as an independent chord acting as a substitute for the V_7 chord.

STRUCTURE AND USE

Although all of the tones in the diatonic scale are included in the complete V_{13} chord, the root, third, seventh, and thirteenth are used in the V_{13} in four-part harmony. The interval of the thirteenth is actually the third degree of the scale and usually appears in the soprano voice. The thirteenth may serve as an accented non-harmonic tone which resolves to the fifth of the V_7 chord. Each chord marked "x" in the excerpt below is formed by an *appoggiatura*. Both analyses are given.

Example 14–16.   SCHUBERT, Sonata, Op. 120 (2nd movement).

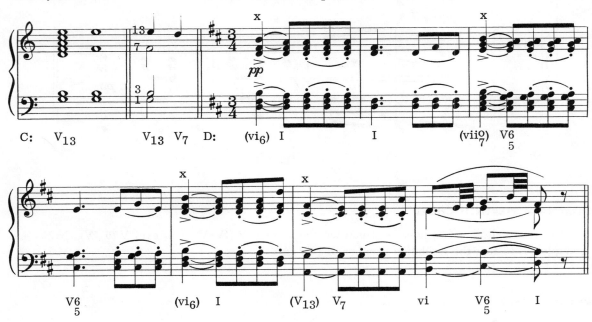

In the normal resolution of the V_{13} to I, the root, third, and seventh resolve as in the V_7, and the thirteenth, being the third of the scale, usually skips down an interval of a third to the tonic tone. The V_{13} is equally effective in major and minor.

Example 14–17.

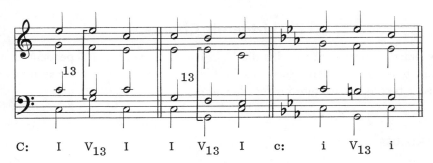

Other possible resolutions of the interval of the thirteenth are (a) to carry over the thirteenth which becomes the third of the resulting I chord with doubled root and third, and (b) to skip up a third from the thirteenth to the fifth of the I chord of resolution.

Example 14–18.

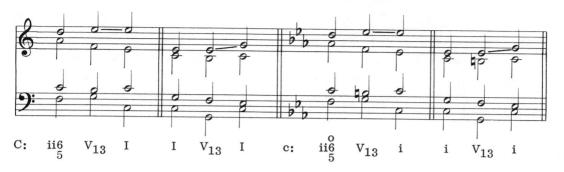

INVERSIONS

While the V_{13} is nearly always found in root position, two inversions are possible, the first and the third. This is because the third and the seventh of the chord, being the bass notes of these two inversions, are the only other tones included in the chord besides the root and the thirteenth. The resolution of the inverted V_{13} is similar to that of the inversions of V_7.

Example 14–19.

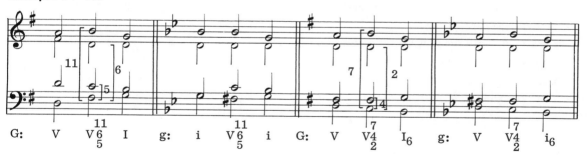

Writing for Three Lower Voices

The category of lower voices includes male voices and also instruments which have a tenor and bass range. The principles presented here apply to both voices and instruments. The possible range of instruments will, of course, be greater than that of singing voices.

Lower voices produce more audible overtones than treble voices, so there must be more care in the arrangement and spacing of the notes in harmony. As in the case of the piano, any grouping of notes in close proximity in the lower range will produce a thick texture which often results in a lack of clarity. The lower range must have a more open texture than the upper range of the treble.

Learn the following facts regarding this type of writing:

1. In contrast to writing for treble voices, more root position chords should be used, especially in the formation of cadences.

2. Chromatics should be used sparingly as their overuse will produce a texture which is too thick.

3. Overlapping is common in writing for lower voices because of the melodic demands, and each voice may be given a rather wide range. Note in Example 14–20 that the tenor part is written in the treble clef one octave above where it is to sound.

Example 14–20.

4. Variety can be obtained by contrast between open and close position, the use of two parts or even of unison, the use of rests and separate entrances of parts, and, perhaps most important, rhythmic variety.

5. Parallel movement of voices is used here, although a more solid feeling of movement and balance is more important with lower voices than in writing for treble voices.

6. The melody may occur in any of the three voices, although it is most frequently found in the tenor or baritone part.

Assignments

1. Harmonize each of the following progressions in four-part chorale style:

   (a) Key of D: I–V_9–V_7–I–V_9–I
   (b) Key of e minor: i–VI–V_9–V_7–VI–$ii^{\circ 6}_{5}$–V_7–i
   (c) Key of A flat: I–I_{11}–I–IV–V–V_{11}–I (in two ways)
   (d) Key of g minor: i–iv–$ii^{\circ}{}_7$–i_{11}–i
   (e) Key of B: I–IV–ii^6_5–V_{13}–V_7–I–V_{13}–I
   (f) Key of a minor: i–$V^{11}_{\substack{6\\5}}$–i–ii°_6–V–$V^7_{\substack{4\\2}}$–i_6–V^4_3–i

2. Listen to progressions, including phrases of actual music, which include ninth, eleventh, and thirteenth chords and determine, as they are played, the identity and function of each chord.

3. At the keyboard, play and memorize each of the following progressions. Play each progression in any major or minor key, as directed by the instructor.

4. Non-pianists: Play original progressions involving ninth, eleventh, and thirteenth chords in piano style in major and minor keys. Pianists: Play the same in free keyboard style.

5. Harmonize the following figured basses in chorale style, using non-harmonic tones:

(a)

(b)

(c)

(d)

6. Harmonize the following soprano melodies, using examples of ninth, eleventh, and thirteenth chords as well as others studied. These are to be written in chorale style, but in a freer manner than the above exercises.

(a)

(b)

(c)

(d)

(e)

7. Harmonize folk songs or other familiar tunes at the keyboard in piano style, using ninth, eleventh, and thirteenth chords.

8. Write short original exercises in major and minor, using examples of ninth, eleventh, and thirteenth chords.

9. Analyze the following excerpt harmonically and stylistically, commenting on the adaptation of the principles of three-part writing for lower voices as presented in this chapter.

LEO SOWERBY, Norse Lullaby.

10. (a) Write a setting for three lower voices or instruments of a familiar melody or one given by the instructor.

   (b) Harmonize the following melody for three lower voices or instruments in two ways: first with the melody in the upper part and then with the melody in the middle part. The melody as given below may be transposed to a different key to satisfy range requirements.

   BACH, Wie schon leuchtet der Morgenstern.

11. Analyze the following excerpts harmonically and stylistically, noting the ninth, eleventh, and thirteenth chords and their functions in each example.

(a) SCHUBERT, Moment Musical, Op. 94, No. 1.

(b) SCHUMANN, Traumerei, Op. 15, No. 7.

(c) GRIEG, Skip Dance, Op. 38, No. 5.

(d) SCHUMANN, Op. 68, No. 26 (*Andante con espressione*).

(e) SCHUMANN, Papillons, Op. 2, No. 7.

(f) GRIEG, Traveler's Song, Op. 17, No. 13.

(g) SCHUMANN, Hunting Song, Op. 68, No. 7.

(h) CHOPIN, Ballade in F, Op. 38 (two excerpts).

(i) SCHUMANN, Little Romance, Op. 68, No. 19.

12. Write a free composition in any medium, employing examples of ninth, eleventh, and thirteenth chords. (The length of this work is to be determined by the instructor.)

13. Write a free original work for three lower voices or instruments, the length and style to be determined by the instructor.

14. Analyze, bring to class, and discuss music in which ninth, eleventh, and thirteenth chords appear.

15

MODAL ALTERATIONS

The major–minor concept in music has been in general use since the seventeenth century. Music written since that time is basically in either the major or the minor mode. Composers discovered that by incorporating characteristic elements of the minor mode into the major tonality, and vice versa, the result would be a colorful mixture of the two modes, yet the basic tonality would remain unchanged.

In achieving this coloristic change, the parallel minor relationship is used with the result that there is but one tonality. In this the third, sixth, and seventh scale steps may be raised or lowered to conform with the appropriate mode being used.

There are two basic means of achieving this type of simple chromatic alteration; one is called "alternation of modes," and the other is called "mixed modes."

Alternation of Modes

To create color and variety and yet remain within the framework of a given tonality, composers may interchange modes. This is accomplished in several ways; the most frequently used is the repetition of a phrase in the opposite mode or the insertion of new material in a composition in the opposite mode. Although this may be considered to be a modulation to the parallel major or minor, no such modulation takes place because the tonality (such as C major and c minor) remains the same.

From the music of Beethoven and Mozart up to that of the twentieth century, this device has been used to good advantage. In some instances it is used to provide relief from one mode; in others, to give more vitality to the repetition of a phrase or to anticipate a modulation. The principal requirement in the alternation of modes is that the mode being used for contrast is maintained long enough to be established in the mind of the listener. No specific duration is required, but certainly one altered chord will not comprise an alternation of mode. The example below illustrates the use of this device:

Example 15–1. SCHUBERT, Allegretto.

Mixed Modes

In contrast to the alternation of modes, "mixed modes" deals with the chromatic alteration of one or two tones in a chord, affecting only one or possibly two chords, rather than an entire phrase which would then establish the key. Thus we find a single altered chord formed by a mode different from that of the existing harmonic framework.

Example 15–2. CHOPIN, Mazurka, Op. 7, No. 4.

iv6♭   vii°7♭
   4

CHORD CONSTRUCTION

The mixing of modes is the result of the use of chromatic passing tones, *appoggiaturas* and other non-harmonic tones in which these chromatic tones become actual chord tones in the harmonic scheme.

Example 15–3.

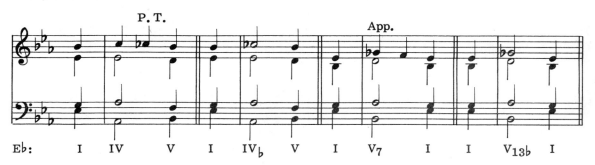

E♭:   I   IV   V   I   IV♭   V   I   V₇   I   I   V₁₃♭   I

For the present, the third, sixth, and seventh scale steps may be lowered in major and raised in minor to achieve this mixing of modes, while the first, second, fourth, and fifth scale steps remain the same in either major or minor. Example 15–4 illustrates the possibilities when altering the third, sixth, and seventh steps in major and minor. The secondary dominant chords as well as the leading tone diminished and half-diminished seventh chords are indicated because of their special function.

Example 15–4.

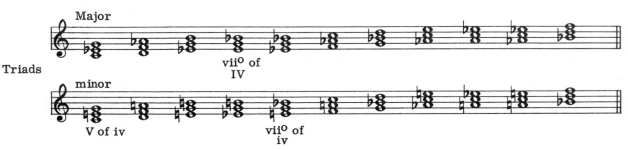

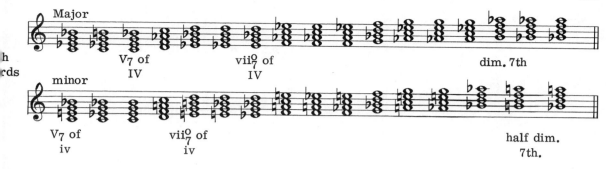

A chord altered in this manner must contain raised or lowered degrees of the scale. Although there are no specific considerations regarding their position within the phrase, these altered chords will assume the same function within the phrase as the diatonic chords from which they have been formed.

HARMONIC APPROACH

An altered chord of this type is approached as though it were an unaltered chord. The altered tone or tones within the chord should be approached smoothly, either from the same tone in its unaltered form or by stepwise motion. Exceptions to this, involving approach by a skip, are possible where the heightened effect of the altered tone is desired.

Example 15–5.

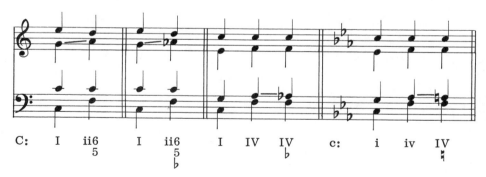

DOUBLING

Principles of doubling in an altered chord are basically the same as those in the unaltered form of the chord. One exception, however, is that the altered tone or tones, being active, are seldom doubled as there is enough interest and color in the altered tone to produce the desired effect. The other exception is that the altered root of the chord may be doubled, thereby producing harmonic stability.

Example 15–6.

RESOLUTION

Use normal principles which apply to diatonic progressions for the resolution of altered chords. Keep in mind that chromatically *raised* tones should resolve *upward* and chromatically *lowered* tones should resolve *downward*, although on occasion the reverse is possible. In each altered chord there should be a musical reason for a tone or tones being altered. Each of these tones should have a logical feeling of movement and destination.

Example 15–7.

CROSS-RELATION

When a tone in its unaltered and altered form in adjacent chords appears in two different voices rather than in the same voice, cross-relation (sometimes called "false relation") occurs. The presence of cross-relation is contrary to principles of good voice leading, and is to be avoided. Exceptions to this occur when two forms of the minor scale are used simultaneously in two voices and also when a composer wishes to create a particularly striking effect of a dissonant nature. Under certain musical circumstances, cross-relation may exist between two different chords if the tones involved do not occur in outer voices.

Example 15–8. BACH, Warum betrubst du dich; BACH, Ihr Gestirn', ihr hohlen Lufte.

FREQUENCY OF USE

If these altered chords appear often enough actually to reverse the prevailing mode for possibly a phrase, the result will be alternation of modes, discussed earlier in this chapter. The use of mixed modes is most effective when used sparingly so that one or two altered chords color a particular progression and give it added interest.

The alterations usually occur in one or two voices, are more frequently used in major keys than in minor, and are most successful if used during a phrase rather than at the beginning or at the end.

Specific Considerations

ALTERED THIRD STEP

1. *Picardy Third* (*tierce de Picardie*) refers to the raised third in the final tonic of a composition in a minor key. The use of this major tonic chord at the end of a work in minor began about 1500 and was widely used during the baroque period. Its purpose was to create a more consonant, positive conclusion to a work written in a minor key.

Example 15–9. BACH, Zeuch ein zu deinen Toren.

final
phrase

a:

2. The most frequently used lowered third scale step in major keys is that of the fifth of the lowered VI triad. In this instance VI becomes a major triad in a major key, contains two altered tones (its root and fifth), and provides a welcome change from the minor vi.

Example 15–10.

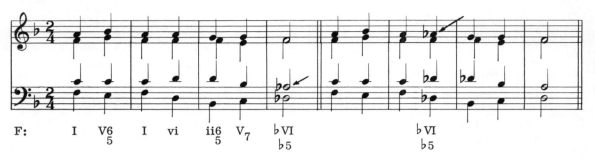

Another lowered third scale step in major is found in the use of a minor tonic chord. While used often in the alternation of modes to establish an opposite mode, it is seldom used in mixed modes independently, although it creates an element of surprise and a darker color when used. Example 15–11 illustrates this device. Notice that attention is called to the lowered third scale step in a melodic manner.

Example 15–11. SCHUBERT, Impromptu, Op. 90, No. 1.

ALTERED SIXTH STEP

In major keys the lowered sixth scale step is used in the alteration of ii and ii$_7$, IV and vi. The ii$_7$, when altered, becomes a half-diminished seventh chord with much warmth and is usually a more successful altered chord than ii. The IV, when altered, becomes a minor triad which particularly softens the effect of basic progressions. The altered vi, already discussed in the preceding section, is unique in that there are two altered tones, the root and fifth of the chord (sixth and third scale steps). (See Example 15–10.)

Example 15–12. Bach, Christus, der ist mein Leben.

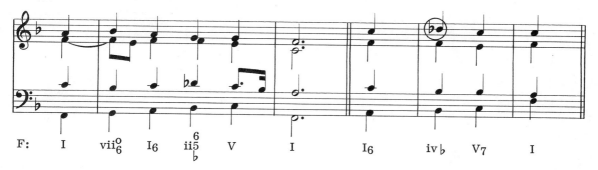

In minor keys, the sixth scale step is sometimes raised in ii and iv to create a smooth melodic line from the sixth to the seventh degrees, or, less frequently, from the seventh to the sixth degrees, thus utilizing the melodic form of the minor scale.

Example 15–13. Bach, Wir Christenleut'.

The ninth of the V_9 and the seventh of the vii_7 can be lowered in major and raised in minor to create another effective alteration of the sixth scale step.

ALTERED SEVENTH STEP

Although the lowering of the leading tone in major usually results in the formation of a secondary dominant chord (V_7 of IV), it may also be used to soften the seventh scale step when harmonized by a V chord. Example 15–14 illustrates the primary use of the lowered seventh scale step in minor: formation of the descending form of the minor scale.

Example 15–14.

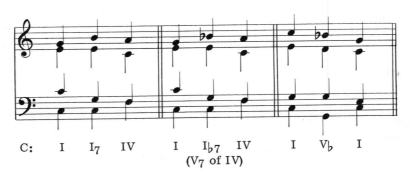

C: I   I₇   IV   I   I♭₇   IV   I   V♭   I
              (V₇ of IV)

Example 15–15. BACH, Für Freuden lasst uns springen.

Writing for Four Treble Voices

At this point it will be beneficial to review the basic principles in Chapter 12 regarding writing for three treble voices, for there are many similarities. The following sections refer more specifically to writing for four treble voices.

COMPLETE CHORDS

While in three-part writing only complete triads or incomplete seventh chords are possible, in four-part treble writing all of the seventh, ninth, eleventh, and thirteenth chords are possible because of the added tone. Doubling principles remain the same as in writing for mixed voices with the exception of the limitations of range in singing voices.

Example 15–16.

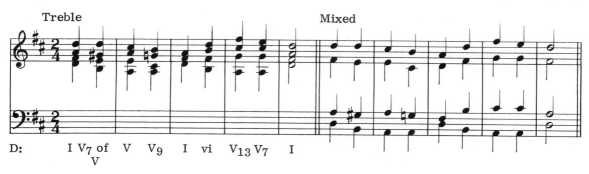

D: I V₇ of V V₉ I vi V₁₃ V₇ I
         V

MOVEMENT OF VOICES

Here the general principles for mixed voices are used—contrary motion, smooth voice leading, etc. Non-harmonic tones may be used to advantage for the stimulation of movement of individual voices.

Contrapuntal technique is less successful here than in writing for mixed voices, for there is such a similarity of tone quality in women's voices (or treble instruments of the same family) that the effect of each individual line will not be heard clearly if too much of this technique is present. The chord approach is more satisfactory, therefore.

Parallel movement, or even seventh chords in succession, is sometimes effective, provided there is a musical reason for this and if the procedure is not overdone.

Example 15–17.

CHORD ARRANGEMENT

As in three-part writing, inversions are successful from the standpoint of interest and lightness of tone quality. The movement of voices is the same as for four-part mixed voices, the range and key determine the extent of chords in root position, and writing in close position is often effective.

Example 15–18.

ACCOMPANIMENT

Because of the sameness in sound and the lack of variety in tone color, an accompaniment is desirable for this medium if the work is of any considerable length. Also, an accompaniment makes more freedom possible in the voices, especially in the second alto part or its equivalent, which otherwise would be limited to a more basic part in the chord structure.

In four-part treble music, as in other media, fewer than four parts will give variety in texture. Here an accompaniment will add fullness and contrast.

Below are two examples of four-part treble writing, one with accompaniment and the other *a cappella*. Study these, using the above points as a guide.

Example 15–19. BRYE, Lewis and Clark.

Example 15–20. PROTHEROE, The Shadow March (*a cappella*).

All round the house is the jet black night, It stares thru' the win-dow pane,___ It

crawls in the cor-ner, hid-ing from the light, And it moves with the mov-ing

flame.___

Assignments

1. Prepare and play a folk tune or simple song for the class, repeating each phrase in the opposite mode for practice in the alternation of modes.

2. Select recently completed exercises, then rewrite, creating altered chords out of unaltered chords where the musical effect can be improved. Experiment with the alterations discussed in this chapter and sing different parts in their unaltered and altered forms.

3. Harmonize the following in chorale style, using altered chords as presented in this chapter. Non-harmonic tones may also be included.

(a)

(b)

(c)

4. Harmonize the following melodies in free keyboard style, using examples of altered chords:

(a)

(b)

5. Write an accompaniment to the following melody in any style, employing the principles of alteration:

6. Listen to progressions, including phrases of actual music, employing modal alterations as they are played, and determine the nature of the alterations.

7. Non-pianists: Play original progressions involving modal alterations in piano style in major and minor keys. Pianists: Play the same in free style.

8. Harmonize folk songs or other familiar tunes at the keyboard in piano style, creating modal alterations where they will be effective.

9. Analyze Examples 15–19 and 15–20 as in previous chapters, commenting on the adaptation of the principles for four-part writing as presented in this chapter.

10. (a) Write a setting for four treble voices or instruments of a familiar melody or one given by the instructor.

   (b) Harmonize the following melody for four treble voices or instruments in free style. If written for instruments, the range may be wider and more contrapuntal movement may be used. This melody may be transposed.

Folk Song

11. Analyze the following excerpts, noting particularly the use of modal alterations:

   (a) MOZART, Fantasie in c minor (K475) (two excerpts).

(b) KABALEVSKY, The Clown.

(c) GRIEG, Waltz, Op. 12, No. 2.

(d) SCHUBERT, Impromptu, Op. 142, No. 2.

(e) BEETHOVEN, Sonata, Op. 53 (*Allegretto moderato*) (3rd movement).

(f) Schumann, Papillons, Op. 2 (part 5).

(g) Tchaikowsky, Reverie.

(h) MENDELSSOHN, Song Without Words, Op. 30, No. 3.

12. Write an original composition for solo voice or instrument with piano accompaniment in which modal alteration is used. (The length of this work is to be determined by the instructor.)

13. Write an original work for four treble voices or instruments in which modal alterations are used.

14. Analyze, bring to class, and discuss music which includes modal alteration. Also bring for discussion works for four treble voices or instruments and perform them.

16

ADVANCED MODULATION

In analyzing the key relationships in music from the time of Bach to the present, we soon realize that many modulations occur which are not of the pivot chord variety. These other types we will refer to as advanced modulations.

To summarize, the pivot chord modulation, discussed in Chapter 10, involved a diatonic chord which was common to both the original key and the key of destination. In succeeding chapters, new possibilities for pivot chord modulation were presented, namely the secondary dominants and the diminished seventh chords.

The following types of modulation are particularly valuable in modulation to remote keys, and it should be kept in mind that the type of modulation to be used will often be determined by the style and idiom of the composition.

MODULATION BY MODAL ALTERATION

In Chapter 15, "Modal alterations," devices of a chromatic nature were presented which can successfully be used as means of modulation. An altered chord may be a pivot chord in a modulation in the following three ways:

1. An altered chord in the original key may be an unaltered chord in the new key.

Example 16–1.

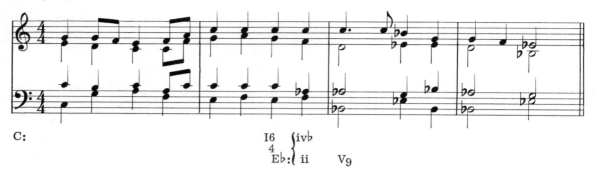

C:

16
4
Eb: { ivb
       ii   V9

2. An unaltered chord in the original key may be an altered chord in the new key.

Example 16–2.

F:

V { iii
E: { iv♮   V7

3. An altered chord in the original key may be an altered chord in the new key.

Example 16–3.

E:

I { iv♮
D: { v♮   vi

ENHARMONIC MODULATION

In this type, one or more tones in a given chord are changed by name (enharmonic notation), these tones becoming other scale steps in the new key. This type of modulation is useful in modulating to remote keys. The diminished seventh chord best illustrates this type of modulation because of its flexibility in regard to key center (see discussion in Chapter 13).

In the last half of the third measure in Example 16–4, the root of the vii°$^6_5$ in e minor which is D sharp in the soprano voice becomes E flat (although not so notated here) in the following measure, the same note now being the seventh of vii°$_{7°}$ in G major.

Example 16–4. Beethoven, Sonata, Op. 2, No. 2 (*Allegro vivace*).

The V$_7$ chord may be used for this type of modulation as well as the augmented fifth and augmented sixth chords, which will be discussed in Chapter 17.

MODULATION BY SEQUENCE

The repetition of a pattern on a different degree of the scale, each repetition appearing in a different key, is an effective means of modulation. The keys involved are usually closely related, often moving in fifths. The effectiveness of this type of modulation depends on the simplicity of the pattern and the relationship of the keys involved. No pivot chord as such is present because the unity is gained through the use of the pattern.

Example 16–5. Beethoven, Sonata, Op. 10, No. 1 (*Allegro molto e con brio*).

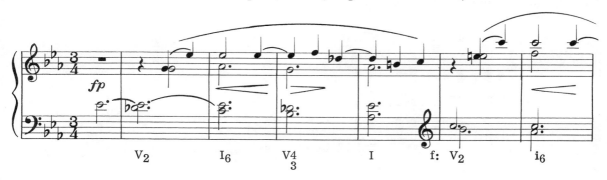

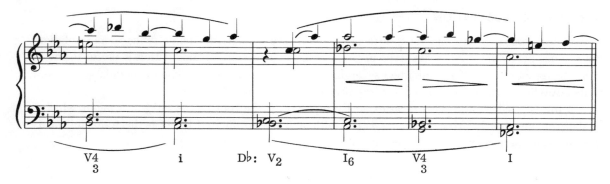

COMMON TONE MODULATION

Sometimes the only connecting link between two different keys will be a single tone which is common to two chords, one in each key. This tone is often found in the soprano voice where the transition can be easily heard. It is also found in an inner voice, and, in its more subtle form, occurs in one voice in the original key and in a different voice in the new key. Although it may appear within a phrase or between two phrases, it is more often used in going from one principal section of a composition to another.

Example 16–6.

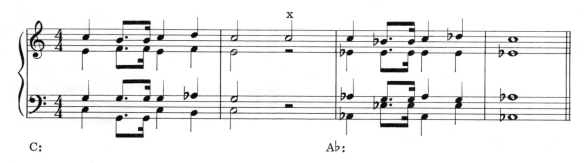

Example 16–7. SCHUMANN, Fantasia, Op. 17.

CHROMATIC MODULATION

In this type of modulation the transition from one key to another is made by moving voices (preferably more than one voice) from a chord of one key to a chord of another. Normal voice leading tendencies will not be observed here, as the modulation will often be to a remote key. The use of non-harmonic tones in the transition assists in developing a more musical feeling because it emphasizes the linear action.

Example 16–8.

ABRUPT MODULATION

In this more extreme type of modulation, where there is no pivot chord or common tone, the new key is introduced with no harmonic warning and with no preparation. This type is used to create an element of surprise, force, or sudden change of mood. In a sense, no modulation takes place because there is no obvious connection between the two keys. However, the rhythmic aspect of the music is important here because the change of tonality usually takes place at the beginning of a phrase or section. While the dynamics indications may vary greatly in each of the two keys, the harmonic and melodic aspects may remain similar.

Example 16–9. SCHUBERT, Moment Musical, Op. 94, No. 2.

Example 16–10. SCHUBERT, Moment Musical, Op. 94, No. 2 (harmonic outline).

Writing for Four Lower Voices

There is very little to be added to the discussion in Chapter 14 under "Writing for Three Lower Voices," in considering writing for four male voices or four lower instruments. The principles are the same, the problems are the same; the only differences are as follows:

1. Because the fourth voice has been added, principles of doubling and chord construction will be similar to those of four-part mixed writing.
2. The melodic part will usually occur in the first or second tenor part more frequently than in the other voices.
3. Care must be exerted to avoid a texture which is too thick in the lower part of the range.

Examples 16–11 and 16–12 illustrate this type of writing.

Example 16–11. LAVERTY, Psalm 117 (TTBB).

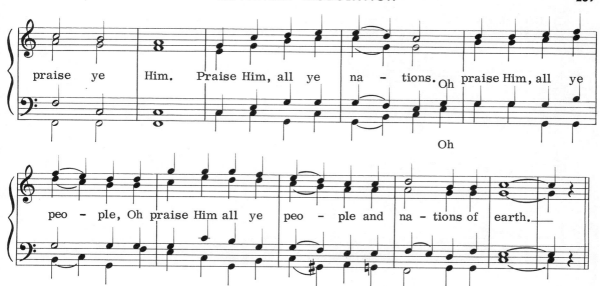

praise ye Him. Praise Him, all ye na - tions. Oh praise Him, all ye

peo - ple, Oh praise Him all ye peo - ple and na - tions of earth.

From Octavo No. 3508—Psalm 117 by John Timothy Laverty. Used by permission of the publishers, Schmitt, Hall & McCreary Company, Minneapolis, Minn.

Example 16–12. MacDowell, Cradle Song, Op. 41, No. 1.

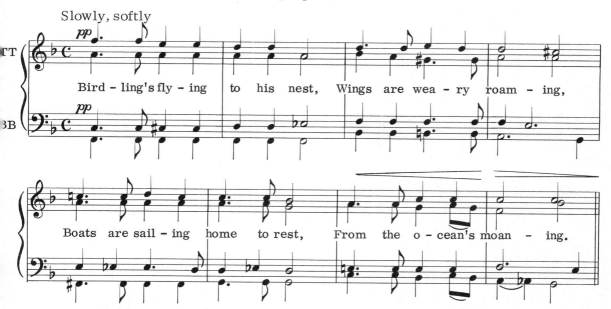

Bird - ling's fly - ing to his nest, Wings are wea - ry roam - ing,

Boats are sail - ing home to rest, From the o - cean's moan - ing.

Assignments

1. By listening to progressions, including phrases of actual music, determine the type and nature of the modulations heard.

2. Harmonize the following in chorale style, using non-harmonic tones and modal alterations where desirable. Indicate the type of modulation being used in each exercise.

(a)

(b)

(c)

3. Non-pianists: Play progressions which modulate by each of the methods discussed in this chapter, in choral or keyboard style. Pianists: in addition, use non-harmonic tones and modal alterations.

4. Write, in chorale style, one original exercise demonstrating each of the types of advanced modulation.

5. Analyze Examples 16–11 and 16–12 as in previous chapters. Comment on the adaptation of principles in this type of writing.

6. Write a setting for four lower voices or instruments of a familiar melody or one selected by the instructor.

7. Harmonize the following melody for four lower voices (TTBB). The melody as given may be transposed to a different key if advisable.

BACH, Nun komm, der Heiden Heiland.

8. Analyze the following excerpts, noting particularly the type of modulation employed and the style of composition:

(a) BACH, Es ist das Heil uns kommen her.

(b) Bach, Warum betrubst du dich, mein Herz.

(c) Mozart, Fantasie in c minor (K475).

(d) BEETHOVEN, Sonata, Op. 53 (1st movement).

(e) BRAHMS, Ballade, Op. 118, No. 3 (two excerpts).

(f) Chopin, Ballade No. 2 in F Major, Op. 38.

(g) Beethoven, Sonata, Op. 13 (1st movement).

9. Analyze, bring to class, and discuss music which includes the types of modulation presented in this chapter.

10. Determine the harmonic rhythm of one of the works discussed in the preceding assignment, then write an original free work on this harmonic rhythm.

11. Write a free composition in any medium in which you employ at least one type of advanced modulation. (The length is to be determined by the instructor.)

17

CHROMATIC
ALTERATION

The simplest types of chromatic alteration are those found in the secondary dominant chords, discussed in Chapter 11, and in the mixing of major and minor modes, discussed in Chapter 15. But there are limitless other possibilities for chromatic alteration. Theoretically, any tone or tones in any given chord may be raised or lowered, each alteration producing a chord which sounds different from the same chord in its original, unaltered form. Depending on their use, these altered tones may consist of non-harmonic tones or may be essential chord tones.

Composers from the common practice period to the twentieth century have made use of chromatically altered chords, the choice and manner of use being determined by the function of such chords, the period in which the work was written, and the style of the particular composer.

Despite the numerous possibilities for altered chords, comparatively few have been in common usage. This is because of the demands placed on tonal music—the basic V to I feeling, the key sense, and the elements of cadence and form. When music extends beyond these ideas by means of chromatic alteration, the key sense is lost and the result is atonality.

To review a point discussed earlier, a chromatically raised tone will usually progress upward and a chromatically lowered tone will usually progress downward. Most of the altered chords resolve to a chord in the original key, although some resolve to another altered chord, thus resulting in ambiguity as far as the feeling of the original tonal center is concerned.

Although we will discover many different types of altered chords in musical analysis, there are certain altered chords which have become so indispensable in musical composition that they must be considered and discussed independently. Those most frequently used are the Neapolitan sixth, the augmented and diminished fifth, the raised ii_7 and vi_7, and the four specific augmented sixth chords.

NEAPOLITAN SIXTH CHORD

This chord, a triad usually in the first inversion, is composed of a major triad built on the lowered second step of the scale. By altering the ii in major or the ii° in minor to conform to this structure, the basic progression of ii_6–V or ii_6–I_4^6 is enhanced by a richer ii chord, thus suggesting the expansion of the tonality.

The Neapolitan sixth chord is formed in minor keys, where it most frequently occurs, by lowering the root of ii°. In major keys, where it is equally effective, it is formed by lowering the root and the fifth of the ii chord. Its normal resolution is to V or I_4^6, the same resolution as that of the unaltered form of ii, but it may also resolve to $vii°_7°$ of V, then to V. While the label for this chord would be $II_6^{6\flat}$ or $II_{6\flat}$, as is frequently used, we will use the label N_6. Note in Example 17–1 that the altered tones follow their tendency and resolve downward.

Example 17–1.

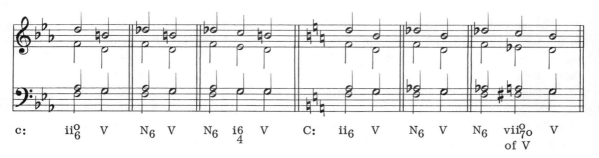

Because it is basically a ii chord and suggests IV because it is usually found in the first inversion, this chord may be preceded by IV, ii, ii_6, vi, or I, in either major or minor keys.

Example 17–2.

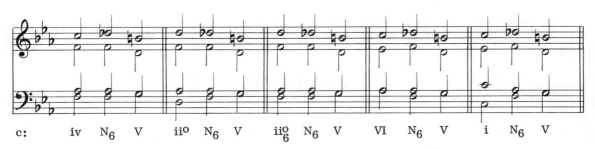

Example 17–3. Chopin, Waltz in a minor, Op. 34, No. 2.

The name of this chord comes from the Neapolitan school of composers, centering around Naples in the late seventeenth and eighteenth centuries. This group is considered by some to be the first to use the Neapolitan sixth chord extensively, but the true source of the chord is the medieval Phrygian mode (see page 9), in which the second degree of the scale is a half step above the keynote.

Although it is most frequently found in the first inversion, which was its original form (hence the name Neapolitan *sixth*), it may be found in root position or even in the second inversion. The figured bass symbols for these other positions are N and N_4^6. While the N_6 has been in use since the seventeenth century, N (root position) is often found in music of the nineteenth century. The altered root is usually doubled when the chord is in root position.

Example 17–4.

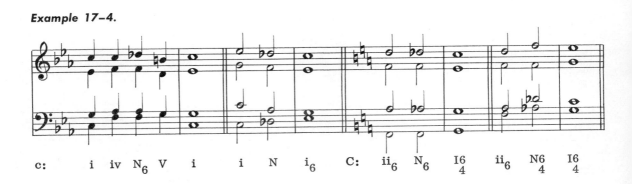

Example 17–5. Chopin, Prelude in c minor, Op. 28, No. 20.

c: i₆ iv V⁶₅ 1 VI Ⓝ V₇ i i

The note to be doubled in this chord is the same note that is doubled in the unaltered ii_6 chord, and normally the altered tone is not doubled. In the progression N_6–V, cross-relation is permissible because of the quality of the progression and because one of the tones is in an inner voice.

Example 17–6.

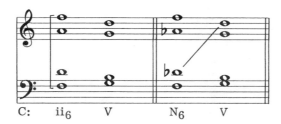

C: ii₆ V N₆ V

The Neapolitan sixth chord is useful as a pivot chord in the enharmonic type of modulation discussed in Chapter 16.

THE AUGMENTED FIFTH CHORD

This chord is restricted to the raising of the fifth of the major triads in major keys (I, IV, V) and the use of the III⁺ in minor keys with the raised leading tone (see page 117). The altered chord may be in root position, in the first inversion, or in a seventh chord and may, in the case of the V chord, be used in V_7 and V_9 as well as in secondary dominants. The raising of the fifth intensifies the chord by leading more directly to the next chord.

The voice leading should be as smooth as possible, with the augmented fifth of the chord resolving upward a half step to a chord tone of the next chord. Other than this statement of voice leading, these chords are approached and left as though they were not altered. When the fifth is raised in the V_7 and the V_9, it is usually placed above the seventh of the chord. Note the irregular doubling in the resolution of the altered V_7 and V_9 in Example 17–7.

Example 17–7.

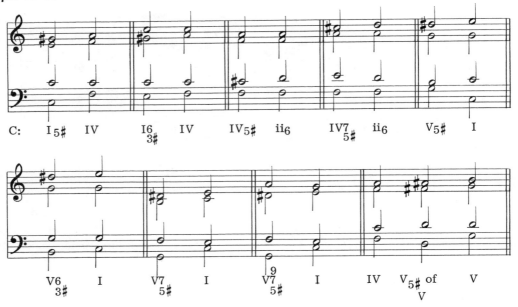

C: I5♯   IV   I6_{3♯}   IV   IV5♯   ii6   IV7_{5♯}   ii6   V5♯   I

V6_{3♯}   I   V7_{5♯}   I   V7_{5♯}⁹   I   IV   V5♯ of   V

Example 17–8. SCHUMANN, Kleine Studie, from "Album for the Young."

G:

THE DIMINISHED FIFTH CHORD

This altered chord, in which the fifth is lowered, is limited to the V and V$_7$ chords. It is more effective in the V$_7$ than in the V, and is especially effective in the V$_3^4$ position, in which the altered tone is in the bass and resolves down a half step to the root of the I chord. The function of this chord remains the same as when unaltered. It may appear in root position or in any inversion, and although it may occur in minor keys, is usually found in major.

Example 17-9.

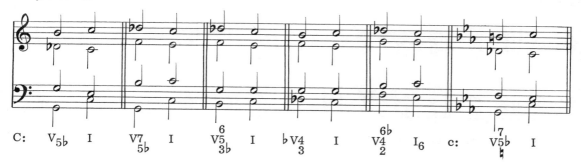

THE RAISED ii°$_{7o}$ AND vi°$_{7o}$

These chords are diminished seventh chords formed by raising the root and third of the diatonic ii$_7$ and vi$_7$ chords in major keys. They are included in this group of altered chords rather than in the discussion of the diminished seventh because these are non-dominant diminished seventh chords in their function and resolution. Those studied in Chapter 13 were vii°$_{7o}$ chords which normally resolved to I.

The raised ii°$_{7o}$ and vi°$_{7o}$ may occur in root position or in any inversion. By resolving the chromatically raised root and third of these chords in the direction of the alteration, the normal chords of resolution will be as follows:

Example 17-10.

While these chords are often preceded and followed by the same chord, thereby creating dependent altered chords, they may be preceded by the unaltered form of the same chords or by chords which would normally progress to the diatonic ii$_7$ and vi$_7$.

Example 17–11.

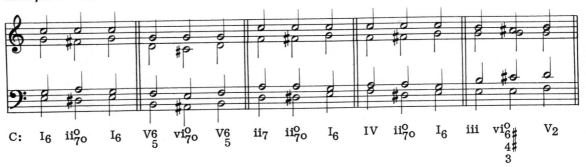

C: I_6 ii^o_{70} I_6 V^6_5 vi^o_{70} V^6_5 ii_7 ii^o_{70} I_6 IV ii^o_{70} I_6 iii $vi^o{}^{\sharp}_{6 4\sharp 3}$ V_2

Example 17–12. BEETHOVEN, Sonata, Op. 53 (3rd movement).

C: ii_7 ii^o_{70}

I_6

Modulation by means of a non-dominant diminished seventh chord is effective and offers one more type of pivot chord modulation. Here the pivot chord will usually be $vii^o{}_{70}$ in the original key and either the raised $ii^o{}_{70}$ or $vi^o{}_{70}$ in the key of destination, although the reverse is possible.

Example 17–13.

D: I ii_6 V_7 I $\begin{cases} vii^o_{70} \\ ii^o_{70} \end{cases}$ I_6 IV V_7 I
B♭:

D: I   ii6   V7   I   Eb: { vii°70 / vi°70 }   V6/5   I   V7   I

The Augmented Sixth Chords

While there are other possibilities for the presence of the interval of the augmented sixth in altered chords, four specific chords which include this interval are discussed here because of their frequency of use and effectiveness. In its usual form, each of these chords contains the characteristic interval of the augmented sixth between the bass note and an upper voice, this interval resolving outward by a half step in each voice to the octave.

The four chords in this group are named the Italian sixth, the German sixth, the French sixth, and the doubly augmented fourth. Each is illustrated in Example 17–14 with the customary figured bass symbol and the name associated with it. It is important to note that all four of these chords have three tones in common; the lowered sixth degree (or simply the sixth degree in minor), the tonic tone, and the raised fourth degree.

Example 17–14.

Italian   German   French   Doubly Aug. 4th

Aug. 6th

C: IV$_{6\sharp}$ IV$5\flat \atop 3$ $^{6\sharp}$ ii$4 \atop 3$ $^{6\sharp}$ ii$4\sharp \atop 3$ $^{6\sharp}$

These chords are basically subdominant in nature, although in sound they resemble V$_7$ chords in their true form or in one case in an altered form. The difference, however, between the augmented sixth chords and the V$_7$ chords lies in their approach and function, and in the notation, which determines the chord of resolution. As with the Neapolitan sixth chord, these chords tend to intensify the motion toward the dominant, and it is for this reason they are valuable.

The augmented sixth chords may be approached from the tonic chord, from the unaltered form of the altered chord, or from a chord which would normally precede it in its unaltered form. The fifth of the chord (the unaltered tone) is doubled in the Italian sixth, but no tone is doubled in the other augmented sixth chords, as they are seventh chords and always are complete.

While they are usually found as illustrated above, that is, the first two being basically IV and the other two ii, it will be discovered as each is discussed that they can be based on other scale degrees than those most commonly used. They are, however, usually found in the inversion as illustrated. These are dramatic chords and should be used sparingly for the best effect.

THE ITALIAN SIXTH (AUGMENTED SIXTH)

This chord, which consists of an altered triad in the first inversion, is most often an altered IV_6. In sound it is identical to an incomplete V_7 in a remote key. If formed from a major triad, the root is raised and the third is lowered (in IV_6 the sixth degree is lowered and the fourth degree is raised). If formed from a minor triad the root is raised (in iv the fourth degree is raised). The chord of resolution is either V or I_4^6. The treatment of the Italian sixth is illustrated below:

Example 17–15.

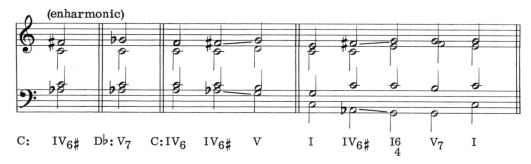

Example 17–16.

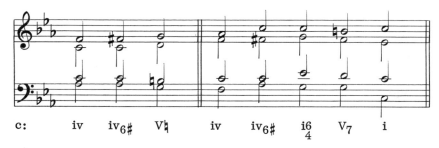

Example 17–17. BEETHOVEN, Sonata, Op. 81a (beginning).

The Italian sixth chord may also appear as an altered ii$_6$ in major or as a vii$_6$ in either major or minor, although these are not common. If formed from a diminished triad, lower the third of the chord (in vii$_6$ the second degree is lowered).

Example 17–18.

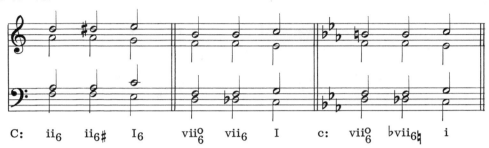

THE GERMAN SIXTH (AUGMENTED $\frac{6}{5}$ CHORD)

Usually appearing as an altered IV$^6_5$ chord, this chord is more restricted in its use and resolution than the Italian sixth. In sound the German sixth chord is identical with that of a complete V$_7$ chord in a remote key, but again the notation is different, demanding a specific resolution. In major it resolves to V, but in minor it may resolve to either V or i$^6_4$. It is formed in exactly the same manner as the Italian sixth chord except that the seventh (placed a perfect fifth above the bass note) is added. Chromatic parallel fifths are permitted here.

Example 17–19.

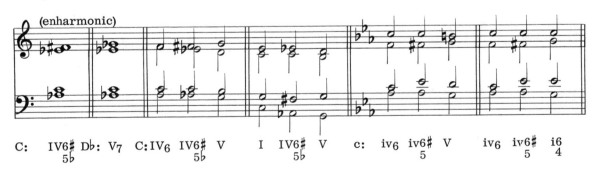

Example 17–20. CHOPIN, Mazurka, Op. 7, No. 2.

Other possible selections for the German sixth chord are the altered forms of the ii$^6_5$ in major or the vii$^6_5$ in major or minor.

Example 17–21.

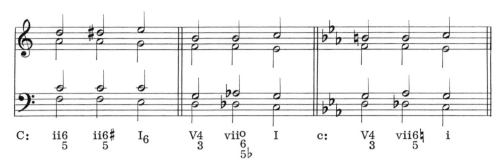

THE FRENCH SIXTH (AUGMENTED $^6_4{}_3$ CHORD)

This is the only augmented sixth chord which in sound is not identical to a V$_7$ of a remote key. Its normal form consists of an altered ii$^4_3$ chord, which may occur in either major or minor keys. Its altered scale degrees are the same as those in the Italian sixth chord, but the addition of the root of the altered ii$^4_3$ places the second degree in the chord (the fourth above the bass note). In major keys the third is raised and the fifth is lowered (the fourth degree raised and the sixth degree lowered), and in minor keys the third is raised (the fourth degree is raised). The resolution of the French sixth chord is to V directly, or indirectly by way of I$^6_4$.

Example 17–22.

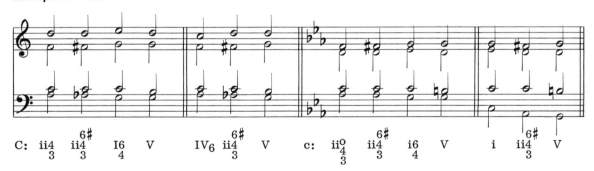

Example 17–23. BEETHOVEN, Sonata, Op. 13 (3rd movement).

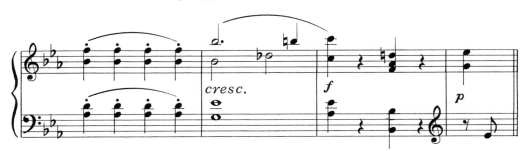

Other possible forms of the French sixth chords are the altered iii$^4_3$ and vii$^4_3$ in major and the altered ii$^4_3$ in minor. Example 17–24 illustrates the necessary chromatic alterations in each case. There are always two augmented intervals in the French sixth chords.

Example 17–24.

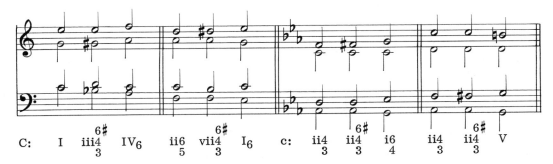

THE DOUBLY AUGMENTED FOURTH

The sound of this chord is identical to that of the German sixth, but the notation of the lowered third degree in the German sixth has been enharmonically changed to the raised second degree. The resolution of the doubly augmented fourth chord is different from that of the German sixth, and the characteristic interval which is responsible for its name is that of a doubly augmented fourth from the lowered sixth degree to the raised second degree in the altered ii$^4_3$, its normal form. This form is possible only in major keys and the resolution must be I$^6_4$.

Example 17–25.

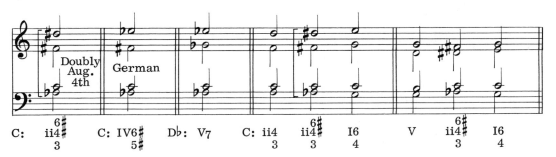

Example 17-26. Chopin, Ballade in A flat, Op. 47.

Limited in its scope, the only other possible forms of this chord are the altered vi$^4_3$ in major and vii$^4_3$ in minor.

Example 17-27.

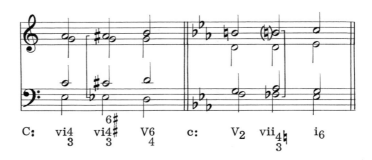

SPECIAL CONSIDERATIONS OF AUGMENTED SIXTH CHORDS

First, it must be pointed out that those which are not normal forms in each type of augmented sixth chord are rarely used. Although the designation of each of these chords indicates the interval of the augmented sixth from the bass note to one of the upper voices, on rare occasions it is possible for each of them to be used either in root position or in other inversions. Example 17–28 reveals some of these possibilities.

Example 17-28.

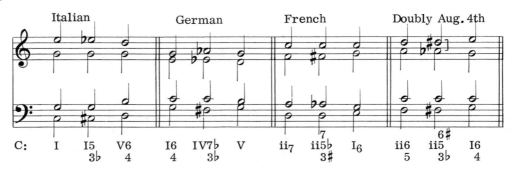

These chords are useful as pivot chords in modulation, because of their V_7 sound. Treated enharmonically, the interval of the augmented sixth becomes the root and seventh of the V_7 chord in the new key.

Assignments

1. Write short progressions in chorale style using one of the following in each: the Neapolitan sixth, augmented fifth, diminished fifth, raised $ii°_7°$, and raised $vi°_7°$. (Keys are to be designated by the instructor.)

2. Listen to progressions, including phrases of actual music, which feature the chords written in assignment 1, and, as they are played, determine the identity and function of each chord. Identify the altered scale step and determine the type of chord being altered.

3. Memorize the basic progressions involving the five types of altered chords listed in assignment 1, and play them in any key, as directed by the instructor.

4. Harmonize the following, using Neapolitan sixth, augmented fifth, diminished fifth, raised $ii°_7°$, and raised $vi°_7°$ chords in chorale style:

(a)

(b)

(c)

(d)

5. (a) Write a short progression in keyboard style, in major, which includes each of the augmented sixth chords. Memorize this progression and play it in any major key.

   (b) Write another progression in minor, using the Italian sixth, the German sixth, and the French sixth chords. Memorize this and play it in any minor key.

6. Spell each of the augmented sixth chords in any key. Sing each of the augmented sixth chords by letter name when the key is given.

7. Identify each of the augmented sixth chords when they are played in progressions.

8. Harmonize the following in chorale or free style, as directed by the instructor, using examples of augmented sixth chords and the other altered chords presented in this chapter. Indicate the name of each altered chord.

(a)

(b)

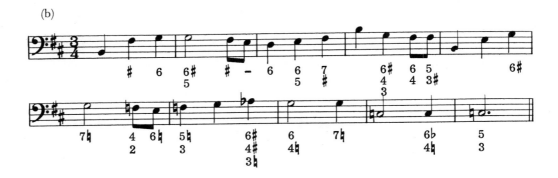

(c)

(d)

(e)

(f)

9. Write, in chorale style, original exercises including the altered chords presented in this chapter.

10. Analyze the following excerpts harmonically and stylistically, naming each of the altered chords and determining the function of each:

(a) BEETHOVEN, Sonata, Op. 31, No. 2 (*Allegretto*).

(b) SCHUMANN, Papillons, Op. 2 (No. 10).

(c) CHOPIN, Nocturne, Op. 15, No. 3 (ending).

(d) SCHUMANN, Volksliedchen, from "Album for the Young."

(e) HELLER, Curious Story.

(f) MENDELSSOHN, Song Without Words, Op. 102, No. 3.

(g) MOZART, Sonata in D (K576) (1st movement).

(h) BEETHOVEN, Variations in c minor (theme).

(i) CHOPIN, Nocturne, Op. 48, No. 2.

(j) BEETHOVEN, Sonata, Op. 53 (2nd movement).

(k) BEETHOVEN, Sonata, Op. 31, No. 3 (1st movement).

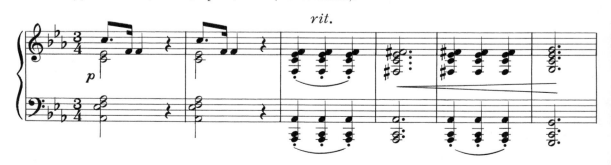

(1) BEETHOVEN, Sonata, Op. 2, No. 1 (1st movement).

11. Analyze, bring to class, and discuss music which includes the types of chromatic alteration discussed in this chapter.

12. Write a free composition in any medium, employing examples of chromatic alteration. Label only the chords presented in this chapter. (The length is to be determined by the instructor.)

CONCLUSION

Throughout the course of this book musical materials have been studied which represent the common practice of composers of the eighteenth and nineteenth centuries. Most of the music of a serious nature which is studied and performed today was composed during that period of time. If this music and its inner structure is understood, it will be possible to study and understand the music of the twentieth century as well as that of the pre-Bach era more easily.

While some may feel that it is impossible to understand fully the music of the twentieth century because the period is too close to us, we must realize that not only has there been much music written in the first two-thirds of this century, but that several broad styles have emerged from the many individual types of writing. While these styles cannot as yet be considered the common practice of our time, they do represent a point of departure as far as the twentieth century is concerned. Atonality, serial writing using the tone row as a basis, neo-classicism, polytonality, and electronic composing represent several of the current trends today. While these involve harmony in one way or another, this new music seems to stress melodic relationships more than those pertaining to harmony. Chords and chord structures are still of importance, but now more in terms of the horizontal aspect. Although comparison of the styles of several composers within a particular musical philosophy is useful, it is more advantageous generally to approach a specific composer or work in its own right.

In studying the style of any particular composer, the initial step should be to understand the general, underlying principles of his period, then to observe how this composer treated these principles by developing them, expanding them, or deviating from them. In the final analysis, principles such as those presented in this book are meant to be *guides* rather than hard and fast *rules* never to be broken. When Debussy rejected nineteenth-century romanticism by employing parallel seventh and ninth chords, the whole-tone scale, and unresolved dissonances, and disposed of the basic V to I cadential pattern, he produced music which was peculiarly his own but which is yet subject to analysis

264

and comprehension despite its irregularities. As it is impossible to divorce oneself from the past, so the study of Debussy, for example, must be undertaken from the standpoint of the period which preceded him.

One must look beyond a single chord, a short harmonic progression, or a bit of melody in studying the music of the twentieth century or any century, and must stand back, in order to see and hear the work as a whole—to understand what a composer has done in the light of the previous common practice. Much fine music has been composed since the turn of the century when perhaps the most radical of all musical changes took place. All serious students of music should explore the wonders of this wealth. Our own time is perhaps the most exciting in the history of musical development.

While the basic principles of music theory in the eighteenth and nineteenth centuries have been presented in this study, it must be left to the student to continue the investigation of music during this span of time, as well as to expand the study to include the music before Bach and since 1900. This will prove to be a meaningful lifetime pursuit.

GLOSSARY OF MUSICAL TERMS

a cappella—for unaccompanied voices.

accelerando—gradually becoming faster.

adagietto—slightly faster than *adagio.*

adagio—a leisurely, slow tempo, faster than *lento* and slower than *andante.*

agitato—in an excited, agitated manner.

alla—in the manner of.

allargando—decreasing in tempo, broadening, and increasing in tone.

allegretto—a lively tempo, not as fast as *allegro.*

allegro—a cheerful, rapid, brisk tempo.

andante—a moderate, flowing, or walking tempo.

andantino—a tempo which is usually a little faster than *andante.*

anima, animato—animated and with spirit.

appassionato—with passion and intensity.

appoggiatura—accented, non-harmonic tone approached by a skip and resolved stepwise.

assai—very.

a tempo—return to the original tempo.

brio—brilliance, life, spirit.

cantabile—in a singing style.

coda—an ending added to a movement or composition.

commodo—comfortable or convenient tempo.
con—with.
crescendo—gradually increasing in loudness.

da capo (D.C.)—from the beginning. The composition is to be repeated from the beginning.
dal segno (D.S.)—from the sign. The composition is to be repeated from the sign.
decrescendo—gradually growing softer.
diminuendo—gradually growing softer.
dolce—sweet and soft.
dolcissimo—extreme of *dolce;* very sweet and very soft.
doppio—double; *doppio movimento*—double speed.

espressivo—with expression.

fermata (⌒)—a hold or pause.
fine—indication of the end of a work after a *D.C.* or a *D.S.*
forte (f)—loud.
forte-piano (fp)—loud, then immediately soft.
fortissimo (ff)—very loud.
fuoco—fire.

giocoso—playful.
giusto—strict and exact.
grave—solemn, serious and slow.
grazioso—gracefully.

-issimo—a suffix meaning "very."

largamente—broadly.
larghetto—not quite so slow or broad as *largo.*
largo—a slow, broad, stately tempo, slower than *lento.*
legato—a smooth and connected manner of playing or singing with no separation between notes.
leggero, leggiero—lightly.
lento—a slow tempo, but not as slow as *largo.*
l'istesso tempo—the same tempo for the beat, although the meter may change.

maestoso—majestically.
marcato—accented, emphasized.
meno—less.
mezzo—half or moderately.
misura—in exact time, measured.
moderato—a moderate tempo.
molto—very or much.
morendo—dying away, growing softer and slower.
mosso, moto—motion.

non—not.

opus—a work, a musical composition. An opus number, such as Op. 13 indicates the order of composition and sometimes of publication of a composer's work.

pesante—heavy, ponderous.
piano (p)—soft.
piu—more.
poco—little; *pochissimo*, very little.
presto—a very fast tempo.
prestissimo—as fast as possible.

quasi—in the manner of, as if.

rallentando—gradually growing slower.
ritardando—gradually growing slower, holding back.
ritenuto—immediately growing slower.
rubato—rhythmic freedom of a beat or measure in which time values are taken from one and given to another for expressive purposes.

scherzando—playfully.
semplice—simply.
sempre—always.
senza—without.
sforzando (sf, sfz, sfp)—forced, a sudden accent.
simile—in the same manner.
smorzando—dying away.
sostenuto—sustained, usually in a fairly slow tempo.
sotto—under, softly.
stringendo—increasing in tempo and intensity.
subito—suddenly.

tenuto—hold, to sustain for its full value.
tranquillo—tranquil and quiet.
troppo—too much.

veloce—swift, fast.
vivace—a quick, lively tempo.
vivo—with life.
voce—voice.

TRANSPOSITION AND TRANSPOSING INSTRUMENTS

Transposition is the procedure of writing, playing, or singing music in a key different from the original. Many of the keyboard exercises in this book call for transposition, the playing of a given progression in various keys. Accompanists are often required to transpose songs so that the music will suit a singer's range. In transposing a melody, scale degrees or intervals should be kept in mind as well as the change of key signature. Where harmony is involved, as in piano music, the harmonic structure of the work should also be analyzed.

Instruments for which the music is written in the same key and octave as that of the actual sound (as on the piano) are said to be playing in "concert pitch." Those instruments for which the music is written in another key or in an octave different from that of their actual sound are called "transposing" instruments. The most commonly used transposing instruments are listed below with the specific transposition described.

B flat clarinet and B flat trumpet or cornet. Key signature is that of a major second above concert pitch. The notes sound a major second lower than written.

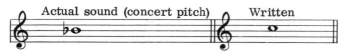

A clarinet. Key signature is that of a minor third above concert pitch. The notes sound a minor third lower than written.

E flat alto saxophone. Key signature is that of a major sixth above concert pitch. The notes sound a major sixth lower than written.

B flat tenor saxophone. Key signature is that of a major second above concert pitch. Notes sound a major ninth lower than written.

E flat baritone saxophone. Key signature is that of a major sixth above concert pitch. The notes sound an octave plus a major sixth lower than written.

English horn. Key signature is that of a perfect fifth above concert pitch. The notes sound a perfect fifth lower than written.

French horn. Key is a perfect fifth above concert pitch. The key signature is not normally used, but all accidentals are written in. Notes sound a perfect fifth lower than written.

C piccolo. Key signature is in concert pitch. The notes sound one octave higher than written.

D flat piccolo. Key signature is a minor second below concert pitch. The notes sound a minor ninth higher than written.

Contrabassoon and string bass. Key signature is concert pitch. The notes sound one octave lower than written.

Various instruments play in the following major keys to correspond to the given concert key.

Actual Concert Key	B flat instrument	A instrument	E flat instrument	F instrument	D flat instrument
C	D	E flat	A	G	B
G	A	B flat	E	D	F sharp (G flat)
D	E	F	B	A	D flat
A	B	C	F sharp (G flat)	E	A flat
E	F sharp (G flat)	G	D flat	B	E flat
B	D flat	D	A flat	F sharp (G flat)	B flat
F sharp (G flat)	A flat	A	E flat	D flat	F
D flat	E flat	E	B flat	A flat	C
A flat	B flat	B	F	E flat	G
E flat	F	F sharp (G flat)	C	B flat	D
B flat	C	D flat	G	F	A
F	G	A flat	D	C	E

SUGGESTED REFERENCE MATERIALS

General.

APEL, WILLI. *Harvard Dictionary of Music.* Cambridge, Mass.: Harvard University Press, 1944.

APEL, WILLI, and DANIEL, RALPH T. *The Harvard Brief Dictionary of Music.* Cambridge, Mass.: Harvard University Press, 1960.

Baker's Biographical Dictionary of Musicians, 5th ed., revised by Nicolas Slonimsky. New York: G. Schirmer, Inc., 1958.

BLOM, ERIC (ed.). *Grove's Dictionary of Music and Musicians,* 5th ed. New York: St. Martin's Press, 1955.

Music Theory and Harmony.

BOATWRIGHT, HOWARD. *Introduction to the Theory of Music.* New York: W. W. Norton & Co., Inc., 1956.

CLOUGH, JOHN. *Scales, Intervals, Keys and Triads.* New York: W. W. Norton & Co., Inc., 1964.

DALLIN, LEON. *Foundations of Music Theory.* Belmont, Calif.: Wadsworth Publishing Co., Inc., 1962.

FORTE, ALLEN. *Tonal Harmony in Concept and Practice.* New York: Holt, Rinehart and Winston, Inc., 1962.

KOHS, ELLIS B. *Music Theory.* Two volumes. New York: Oxford University Press, 1961.

PISTON, WALTER. *Harmony,* 3rd ed. New York: W. W. Norton & Co., Inc., 1962.

SESSIONS, ROGER. *Harmonic Practice.* New York: Harcourt, Brace & World, Inc., 1951.

The Twentieth Century.

DALLIN, LEON. *Techniques of Twentieth Century Composition,* 2nd ed. Dubuque, Iowa: Wm. C. Brown Co., 1964.

MARQUIS, G. WELTON. *Twentieth Century Music Idioms.* Englewood Cliffs, N. J.: Prentice-Hall, Inc., 1964.
PERSICHETTI, VINCENT. *Twentieth Century Harmony.* New York: W. W. Norton & Co., Inc., 1961.

Collections for Analysis.

BURKHART, CHARLES. *Anthology for Musical Analysis.* New York: Holt, Rinehart and Winston, Inc., 1964.
HARDY, GORDON, and FISH, ARNOLD. *Music Literature.* New York: Dodd, Mead & Co., 1963.
MURPHY, HOWARD A., and MELCHER, ROBERT A. *Music for Study.* Englewood Cliffs, N. J.: Prentice-Hall, Inc., 1960.
STARR, WILLIAM J., and DEVINE, GEORGE F. *Music Scores Omnibus.* Two volumes. Englewood Cliffs, N. J.: Prentice-Hall, Inc., 1964.

Two editions of the *371 Chorales* of Johann Sebastian Bach are recommended. One is edited by Albert Riemenschneider and is published by G. Schirmer, Inc., and the other is the reprint of the Breitkopf edition, published by Associated Music Publishers.

INDEX